Mountains to Sound

Text by Daniel Jack Chasan

Foreword by former Washington Governor Daniel J. Evans

Mountains to Sound

The Creation of a Greenway across the Cascades

Photographs by Phil Sturholm,
Larry Hanson, and Other
Northwest Photographers

Mountains to Sound Greenway Trust

Sasquatch Books

Seattle

The Mountains to Sound Greenway Trust wishes to thank the Bullitt Foundation for generously providing funding for this publication.

Library of Congress Cataloging in Publication Data
Chasan, Daniel Jack.
     Mountains to sound : the creation of a greenway across the cascades / Daniel Jack Chasan ; foreword by Daniel J. Evans ; photographs by Phil Sturholm, Larry Hanson, and other northwest photographers.
        p.   cm.
    ISBN 0-912365-83-8 $19.95 (pbk)
    ISBN 0-912365-88-9 $27.00 (hc)
     1. Greenways—Cascade Range.   2. Cascade Range—Description and travel.
I. Title.
F897.C3C47 1993   93-12590
917.9504'43—dc20   CIP

Cover: John Marshall/Allstock, Mount Stuart, Alpine Lakes Wilderness, © 1986 (top); Joel W. Rogers/Allstock, Lincoln Park, Seattle, © 1989 (bottom)
Frontispiece: I-90 near Preston, looking east toward Rattlesnake Mountain
Back cover: I-90 near Cle Elum, looking west

Edited by John P. Pierce
Designed and produced by Marquand Books, Inc.
Typeset using Aldus PageMaker 4.0. © 1985–1991 Aldus Corporation
Text in Adobe Minion; display in Adobe Gill Sans and Franklin Gothic
Printed and bound in Hong Kong by C & C Offset Printing Co., Ltd.

Published and distributed by
Sasquatch Books
1931 Second Avenue
Seattle, WA 98101
(206) 441-6202

Photo and illustration credits
Except where indicated, photographs are by Phil Sturholm. Center for Rural Massachusetts, University of Massachusetts, Amherst, p. 119 (left, right); Johnny Closs/*Seattle Times*, p. 93 (bottom); Larry Dion/*Seattle Times*, p. 93 (top); Peg Ferm, pp. 18–19; Peter Fisher, p. 33; George White Location Photography, pp. 80, 125; Larry Hanson, pp. 10, 13, 38 (top), 39 (right), 78, 86 (top), 118; Jones & Jones, p. 99; Jones & Jones/Seth Seablom, pp. 44, 66, 121; Ann Marshall, pp. 43 (bottom), 83 (bottom), 88; Museum of History and Industry, Seattle, pp. 14, 17, 23, 60; Pemco Webster and Stevens Collection, Museum of History and Industry, Seattle, p. 54, 55 (top); Renton Historical Society and Museum, p. 58; Al Schober, p. 59; Seattle Municipal Archives, p. 65 (bottom); *Seattle-Post Intelligencer* Collection, Museum of History and Industry, Seattle, p. 62, 63; *Seattle Times*, p. 65 (top); Snoqualmie Valley Historical Society, p. 53; UCLA Department of Geography, p. 46; Susan M. Viles-Muzzey, p. 38 (bottom); Washington State Department of Natural Resources, pp. 86 (bottom), 108 (top); Washington State Department of Transportation/Denton Vanderpoel, p. 35, 124; Weyerhaeuser Company, p. 42, 106, 107, 108 (bottom), 110; Weyerhaeuser Company Archives, Clark Kinsey photograph, p. 104

Contents

6   Foreword
Daniel J. Evans

8   Introduction
James R. Ellis

11   **Chapter I**
The View from Mount Si Is Still Green

21   **Chapter II**
From Elk Heights to Elliott Bay

37   **Chapter III**
A Vision of the Greenway

49   **Chapter IV**
A Path Has Always Crossed These Mountains

69   **Chapter V**
Wilderness Close to the City

79   **Chapter VI**
Saving the Issaquah Alps

91   **Chapter VII**
Citizens and Public Money Built a Trail

103   **Chapter VIII**
Commercial Forestry Keeps the Land Unpaved

115   **Chapter IX**
The Challenge to Save Our Future

126   Board of Directors and Technical Advisory Committee

128   Additional Reading

128   Index

Foreword

When Captain George Vancouver explored Puget Sound two hundred years ago, he could see the rugged profile of the Cascade Range to the east. The deep notch of Snoqualmie Pass split the mountains, beckoning to those who would explore the interior. Indian travelers for centuries maintained a trail through the pass, showing the way for the trappers and miners who followed. A trickle at first and then a flood of settlers headed for the shores of Puget Sound using this extraordinary low-elevation gateway. The foot trail widened to accommodate horses, and soon the ring of axes, the thump of shovels, and the curses of workers transformed the route into a wagon road. Territorial legislatures argued incessantly over routes through the Cascades. Eventually, local enthusiasts took over and convinced King County commissioners that a permanent road was vital. The highway was seasonal at first and only barely drivable. But the automobile age had arrived, and a two-lane concrete highway made Snoqualmie Pass the preferred route through the Cascades. World War II halted highway development, but in the 1950s the federal interstate system was created. The Indian footpath of two centuries earlier became Interstate 90. This transcontinental highway not only carries interstate traffic but serves the rapidly spreading suburbs of Seattle. Population growth demands space, so housing and industry spread like an amoeba toward the mountains along major transportation arteries. It took five generations of builders to construct this vital route. It may take only one to destroy the natural beauty through which it passes. Fortunately, many Washingtonians use I-90 to get to the mountains, not through them. We ski, hike, hunt, fish, and just savor the beauty of this extraordinary corridor.

I remember vividly my first hike near Snoqualmie Pass. Our scout troop climbed Silver Peak on a cold, wet November day. Rain turned to snow as we slogged up the mountainside. I alternately wondered why I was there and how I was going to get down. There was no question that this would be the last venture in the wilderness for this tenderfoot scout. But a strange transformation took place as we straggled to the top of the peak. We stood shivering in the cold, surrounded by the dull-gray fog, yet exulting in the success of the climb. I knew I would come back, the next time to see what I could then only imagine. That began a fifty-year love affair with the mountains and wilderness of Washington.

I remember, too, as a sophomore at Roosevelt High School, joining a work party to plant trees on a barren hillside just west of Snoqualmie Pass. It was one of the early reforestation efforts on clearcut lands. Teenagers don't have a long time horizon, so I gave little thought to the future forest we were creating. But now it's a thrill to drive past a thick, tall growth of mature trees a half century old.

Thousands of Washingtonians share similar experiences. We all use this remarkable corridor but want to preserve its unique natural spaces so close to our urban centers.

We also share two other important attributes: a rare willingness to volunteer on behalf of important causes, and a unique ability to find creative solutions to seemingly intractable problems.

The Mountains to Sound Greenway Trust combines these qualities to an unusual degree. Dedicated volunteers are crafting a comprehensive preservation program. The goal is not just a scenic parkway along I-90 from Elk Heights to Seattle. It's also to protect working farms and forests, retain identities of local communities, and to provide outdoor recreation to residents and tourists.

Join me in reading this remarkable account of a historic region. I hope its message will encourage your support to make the Mountains to Sound Greenway a reality.

Daniel J. Evans

Introduction

This book has been published to help Washington residents and visitors appreciate and enjoy a national treasure that lies at their doorstep. The Snoqualmie Pass highway is our workhorse transportation route through the Cascade Mountains. In 1990 it carried forty-three million tons of freight and fifteen million people. Few of its travelers, however, know very much about the exciting history and natural wonders they are passing through.

An interstate highway is both a great help and a potential threat to the enjoyment of natural landscapes. It can bring to the edge of our cities the "good tidings" that John Muir found in remote mountains. It can be every person's doorway to the natural world. Metro buses can deliver people of all incomes and physical conditions to trailheads on Interstate 90 for a day of peace in forested hills or beside rivers and lakes.

High-speed expressways, however, are also noisy and frenetic, and they attract urban development like a pied piper. Unless we plan carefully, the scenic beauty, the working farms and forests, and the distinctive communities along this route could be smothered piece by piece under the next wave of urban growth. A few years later, a strip city may stand where forests grow today.

Some of your fellow citizens are working to save portions of this route in King and Kittitas counties as a scenic legacy. We want to preserve the native plants, the birds and animals, the natural landmarks, the productive farms and forests, and the individual identities of the communities along the way. We believe that a permanent greenway in this corridor will increase the number of good jobs and the value of urban development on both sides of the Cascade Mountains. It will surely enrich the opportunities for recreation and education.

Working forests form the basic character of this greenway. We believe that skillful forestry can profitably grow and selectively harvest Douglas fir trees and still keep green vistas, safeguard watercourses, and enhance outdoor recreation. Sustained-yield practices and new recycling processes can meet society's long-term need for wood and paper products while conserving forested land.

Where natural monuments exist, we believe that a collective public effort should protect them. Already, actions have been taken by the state Department of Natural Resources and the Weyerhaeuser Company to permanently preserve Mount Si. The Trust for Public Land now holds an option to acquire Rattlesnake Ridge, and the state Parks Department plans to expand Squak Mountain and Olallie parks. The national forest service recently established a "visual management" regime to regulate logging in the greenway viewshed. The counties and cities are diligently pursuing open space programs that will strengthen their systems of trails and parks in the corridor.

Prior generations invested wisely in our parks, trails, wilderness, and recreation areas. By connecting these islands of public park and forest-land, we can multiply their recreational and resource value and protect wild-life habitat and corridors of safe movement.

A greenway from the mountains to the sound can bring outdoor classrooms within reach of urban residents of all ages. It can illustrate great lessons from natural history and the contributions of many races of people to our Northwest way of life. The conservation ethic that respects all forms of life may find its way into our turbulent cities.

To realize a greenway-parkway in this corridor will require more of the same kind of landscaped roadways that Washington's farsighted Department of Transportation has built in some new sections of the interstate. As older pavements wear out, they can be rebuilt to parkway standards. Oncoming traffic can be visually separated, and safe underpasses for wildlife and safe paths for hikers and bikers can be constructed.

Of course, the benefits available to local residents can also be enjoyed by visitors. Our rich environment brings tourism, and an attractive greenway may pay for itself in new revenues generated by the hospitality industry.

The Bullitt Foundation and the Mountains to Sound Greenway Trust jointly commissioned Dan Chasan and Phil Sturholm to tell the story of the Mountains to Sound Greenway in words and pictures. As you read through this book you will enjoy its portraits of man-made and natural landscapes and its vignettes of travel and romance. We hope you will fall in love with this Northwest gateway and actively embrace our dream for a greenway from Elk Heights to Puget Sound along the much loved Snoqualmie Pass highway.

James R. Ellis, President
Mountains to Sound Greenway Trust

Jim Ellis, on the right, and his brother Bob at their cabin near the Raging River, 1937.

Looking out from Little Si, it's hard to imagine that you're standing near the edge of the Northwest's largest metropolitan area: downtown Seattle lies less than thirty miles away. You can barely make out the eight-lane ribbon of concrete, I-90, that carries fifteen million people a year east and west across Snoqualmie Pass.

Chapter I

The View from Mount Si Is Still Green

The brilliant infield green of new grass in the pastures far below is broken by darker patches of trees, the winding paths of rivers, the clumped buildings of small towns. Beyond the valley rolls a solid line of forested ridges, dark green with firs and hemlocks and—hidden in ravines filled with cool air and the sound of rushing water—cedars and moss and ferns. You're standing on solid rock, but the landscape spreads beneath you as if you were looking from an airplane, as if you were a raven riding the air currents below. The towns strung along the riverbanks fade in the distance. The valley widens northwest to the horizon. The freeway on the far side curves around the ridges and disappears. Behind the layer of ridges is another and another, each darker and hazier than the one before.

This landscape doesn't seem especially American; it certainly doesn't seem western—not with this complex patchwork of fields and trees and distinct small towns. It doesn't have the dry soil or wind-blasted rock of the inland plateaus. It doesn't have the faceless sprawl that a lot of people associate with cities in Southern California or Arizona. It could be New England—except for the Gothic crags of gray rock dusted with lichen that frame your vision and the solid line of snowcapped mountains to the west. It could be Europe—except that to the south, looming over the layers of ridges, you see the perfect, white, fourteen-thousand-foot cone of a snowcapped volcano.

The perfect volcano, the Taj Mahal of mountains, is, of course, Mount Rainier, and the landscape is part of western Washington—a very commonplace part, too. The freeway curving along the far side of the valley is I-90, over which some fifteen million people drive to and from Seattle each year. The closest of the rivers, curving green around the base of the mountain at your feet, is the middle fork of the Snoqualmie. The checkerboard of grass and trees stretching to the horizon is the Snoqualmie Valley.

The closest town is North Bend. Next comes Snoqualmie, where you can see the old log yard and the sawdust pile of the Weyerhaeuser Company

Mount Rainier, the Taj Mahal of mountains, is a cherished part of the western Washington landscape.

Each year 1.5 million people visit Snoqualmie Falls, a major natural attraction in the Snoqualmie Valley. Once a traditional gathering place of local Native Americans, Snoqualmie Falls is actually one hundred feet higher than Niagara Falls. Above the falls stands a hydroelectric plant built by the Snoqualmie Falls Power Company at the turn of the century. A powerhouse below the falls was the first completely underground generating facility in the world.

lumber mill. In the distance lies Fall City. You can see a complex writhing of channels where the three forks of the Snoqualmie River come together—the old Weyerhaeuser mill pond, filling what used to be a dry oxbow, complicates the scene—then the channel drops from sight and the whole valley is lower. The drop is Snoqualmie Falls, a sacred spot of the Snoqualmie Indians, who thought—and still believe—the mists that rise when the 268-foot streams of falling water shatter on the rock ascend like prayers to heaven.

Your vantage point is Mount Si, striking when you see it from the freeway thirty miles from Seattle, a continual presence looming over the main streets of North Bend and Snoqualmie and long one of the most popular hiking spots in Washington State. Although the climb is steep—thirty-two hundred feet in four miles, the equivalent of an eighty-story building each mile—everybody climbs it: old people, young people, families with children. Some people climb it a lot: a Kirkland couple wrote to the *Seattle Times* in 1992 that "we conducted an informal survey of hikers as we made our monthly roundtrip . . . on April 5. Many of those surveyed are frequent users of the trail; once a week or more. One couple made eighty-five trips this past year." Early in the morning, early in the season, there may be very few people on the trail: a fit young man running up as he trains for an ultramarathon; a fit old man walking up to celebrate his eightieth birthday; a handful of others. But on a sunny weekend, the parking lot at the base of the mountain is full, and people sprawl across the rocks on top, sunning themselves like a herd of beached sea lions.

There may be no better place to appreciate the regional cult of the outdoors—a 1907 climb of Mount Si was the first mountain hike planned by the Seattle outdoor organization The Mountaineers—and no better vantage point from which to appreciate how much of the valley landscape is still rural, how much of the highlands still undeveloped, how much of the open land still tied together on the edge of the largest metropolitan area in the Pacific Northwest.

Much of the greenway corridor has been shaped for generations by farming and logging and is still a working landscape. The Snoqualmie Valley has long been a major dairy farming area. *Top:* Meadowbrook and Tollgate farms, which date from the late nineteenth century, form an integral part of the rural character of the upper valley. *Bottom:* The land that became Meadowbrook was once the largest hop ranch in the world.

It is still very much a working landscape: you can see clearcuts on the side of Rattlesnake Mountain across the way, and the Weyerhaeuser mill site in Snoqualmie has been processing lumber for seventy-five years. The lower Snoqualmie Valley, stretching to the horizon, is still a major dairy area. This has been farming country for a long time. The fields below form parts of Meadowbrook and Tollgate farms, which date from the late nineteenth century. In the 1880s the land that became Meadowbrook formed part of the largest hop ranch in the world: the ranch spread across the valley, and at harvest time some twelve hundred people—many of them Indians who insisted on being paid in silver coin—showed up to bring in the crops.

The forests aren't what they were then, of course. The old-growth trees you encounter halfway up the Mount Si trail—a huge, dim, silent cathedral grove—are the exception rather than the rule. No one is cutting

Top: This thirteen-foot-diameter cedar log, displayed on a railcar in downtown Snoqualmie, came from an ancient tree cut in 1974. *Bottom:* Old-growth trees are no longer harvested in the I-90 corridor, but logging continues in second- and third-growth forests that cover most of the landscape.

trees like the one felled east of North Bend at the turn of the century that was milled into a single timber four feet square and eighty feet long. The thirteen-foot-diameter cedar log that rests on a railroad car in downtown Snoqualmie came from one of the last big trees cut in this area, in the mid-1970s. The Weyerhaeuser sawmill, originally built to cut old-growth logs, was torn down in 1989, largely because it was hopelessly unsuited to processing smaller second- and third-growth trees. Other buildings on the mill site now dry, sand, and otherwise "finish" lumber milled near Enumclaw.

But forests still cover a lot of the slopes, still contain pockets of old trees, and still provide habitat for a wide variety of wildlife. Behind the nearest ridgeline lies an unbroken swath of green, Seattle's Cedar River watershed. Much of the watershed has been and still is logged, but unlogged portions contain Douglas firs up to seven hundred years old. Closed to hunters and—unless you make special arrangements—the rest of the public, the watershed serves as a de facto wildlife refuge. It contains perhaps six hundred elk, black bears, at least one nesting pair of northern spotted owls, three of

Hiking and biking trails crisscross the Snoqualmie Valley. The John Wayne Pioneer Trail runs through Iron Horse State Park and is managed by the Washington State Parks and Recreation Commission. It begins at Rattlesnake Lake near North Bend and crosses the Cascades into eastern Washington, following the old Milwaukee, St. Paul, and Pacific Railroad right-of-way. There are many places to pick up the trail, including a trailhead at Easton, east of Snoqualmie Pass.

Washington's ten potential breeding pairs of common loons, and probably twenty-five to forty-five cougars. The larger animals fan out into the forests outside the watershed. They have to. Even at ninety thousand acres, the watershed isn't big enough to hold them all the time. The cougars need the most space to roam. Rocky Spencer, who works out of the North Bend ranger station, has found that the average home range of a female cougar is forty thousand acres. For a male cougar, it's ninety thousand acres—and male cougars avoid crossing each other's paths. With ranges that large, the animals have to cover a lot of ground outside the watershed. At least some of the cougars seem to follow the ridgeline all the way to Bellevue at the leading edge of urban sprawl.

People, too, can follow the ridgelines all the way to the city. Although you can't see them from the top of Mount Si, hiking trails crisscross the mountains on the far side of the valley. Other trails lead through the lowlands. Much of the old Milwaukee, St. Paul, and Pacific Railroad right-of-way across the mountains has been converted to the John Wayne Pioneer Trail, which ultimately leads across the state. Another segment of abandoned right-of-way leads five miles from the old logging town of Preston to a spectacular view of Snoqualmie Falls.

This landscape may be a long way from the original forest and prairie in which the Snoqualmies and the first white settlers lived, but it is also a long way from the plastic fast-food signs, asphalt parking lots, and composition-shingle roofs that one expects to see spreading like an oil slick over undeveloped land at the edge of a city. To see this scene in this place at the end of the twentieth century is remarkable. But it is by no means sure that the view from Mount Si will be anything like this in the century to come.

Si itself was not protected as a state conservation area until 1976. The clearcut slopes just east of the summit were not publicly owned until 1990. A lot of the landscape and a lot of crucial connections between wildlife corridors and hiking trails remain unprotected. Plastic signs and faceless warehouse walls already crowd parts of the freeway. Bulldozers are scraping the topsoil around trailheads, and orange stakes show where the bulldozers are likely to come next.

A lot of people have big plans for land that is currently undeveloped. On the East Sammamish Plateau, the developed area doubled from 1981 to 1990, and by early 1992 plans to develop most of the remaining land were making their way through the permit process. Just four companies have plans to develop a total of seven square miles on the Sammamish Plateau. Studies done for the Puget Sound Regional Council suggest that the population east of Lake Sammamish more than doubled during the 1980s and will increase by nearly three-quarters between 1990 and 2010. Population in the Fall City–Preston area is expected to increase by 88 percent over the same time span.

The completion of a new bridge and tunnel linking I-90 to Seattle has made travel along the freeway corridor quicker and easier than it was during the high-growth 1980s. Development has flowed east, and—unchecked—it will continue to flow without regard for the public interest that lies in the views, trails, wildlife habitat, and traditional working landscape.

Snoqualmie River & Mount Si   1100

Even now the view west toward the cities of Bellevue and Seattle is rather ominous: the tops of the Olympic Mountains, on the western horizon, gleam a pure, snow-glare white, the upper slopes an almost glacial blue, but the lower slopes are hidden by a sea of brown smog. You can see the smog as a symbol of what's worst about the city, threatening to spread east across this landscape. Or you can see it as a tangible product of the city that is being channeled out along the freeway corridor. Either way, protecting the landscape as the city and its brown air spread east will be a challenge.

How do we keep the traditional working landscape of logging and farming, the characters and sharp boundaries of the small towns, the continuous bands of forest that allow animals and hikers to walk from the mountains to the edge of the city? How do we preserve the views from the freeway and other roadways on which most people spend hours of their everyday lives? How do we enable people to walk or cycle into—or out of—the heart of the city? How do we create—or preserve—connections among the trails and habitats so they don't become fragments scattered across the landscape?

The goal should be permanent pathways from the far side of the mountains to—and through—the city. Some of these pathways will follow the freeway corridor, others will branch out from it. Together they will save, link, and make accessible places of aesthetic, historical, and environmental significance. Even in the next century, people who follow these pathways will be able to move through an urban population center without losing touch with the natural and historic features that make this place unique.

The view of Mount Si and the Snoqualmie River hasn't changed much since the turn of the century. Making sure we keep the look and feel of the landscape a century from now requires strong community involvement and a commitment to preserving the special character and history of our region.

The Mountains to Sound Greenway begins at Elk Heights on the dry, pine-covered eastern slope of the Cascades, follows the Yakima River close to Lakes Cle Elum, Kachess, and Keechelus, passes through two national forests, and skirts the Alpine Lakes Wilderness. Descending from Snoqualmie Pass to the moist green of the western slopes, the greenway follows the south fork of the Snoqualmie River near the Twin Falls Natural Area, passes by the Weyerhaeuser Company's Snoqualmie tree farm, Mount Si, and Tiger Mountain State Forest, and crosses Lake Washington into the oldest part of Seattle. A drive along the greenway takes less than ninety minutes.

Mountains to Sound

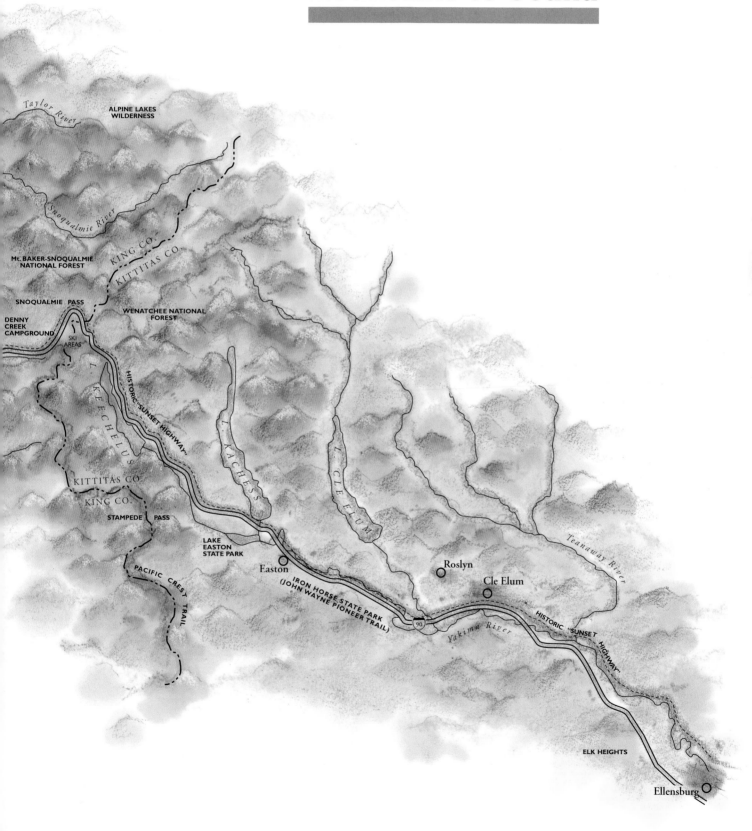

Taylor River

ALPINE LAKES
WILDERNESS

Snoqualmie River

Mt. BAKER-SNOQUALMIE
NATIONAL FOREST

KING CO.

KITTITAS CO.

SNOQUALMIE PASS

WENATCHEE NATIONAL
FOREST

DENNY
CREEK
CAMPGROUND

SKI
AREAS

L. KEECHELUS

HISTORIC "SUNSET HIGHWAY"

L. KACHESS

L. CLE ELUM

Teanaway River

KITTITAS CO.

KING CO.

STAMPEDE PASS

PACIFIC CREST TRAIL

LAKE
EASTON
STATE PARK

Easton

IRON HORSE STATE PARK
(JOHN WAYNE PIONEER TRAIL)

90

Roslyn

Cle Elum

Yakima River

HISTORIC "SUNSET HIGHWAY"

ELK HEIGHTS

Ellensburg

Chapter II

From Elk Heights to Elliott Bay

From the freeway above Issaquah, you get a quick glimpse of an old concrete bridge, green with moss, at the edge of the trees. You don't see the time-shattered, eight-foot stump with new trees growing from its heart. You don't notice that some firs still growing from the bank are three or four feet across. You can't know that the underpass below the bridge on which the freeway crosses a fork of Issaquah Creek is almost certainly a kind of freeway for wildlife; biologists assume that the tunnels formed when the freeway crosses streams between Issaquah and Denny Creek all enable critters to travel north and south without winding up as road kill. You don't see the deer tracks embedded in soft ground along the old road grade. You don't even have time to contemplate the bridge itself, with moss clinging to every ledge, ferns and mossy maple limbs growing toward it—or to reflect on the probability that someday, the eight-lane concrete ribbon of I-90 will itself be a ruin, crumbling in the underbrush while people speed past on something else.

There is a great deal to see from the concrete of I-90, but you don't see many signs of the past. If you climb westward from the dry plateaus of eastern Washington to the pine-covered hills of Elk Heights, you can't miss the white, saw-toothed peaks of ninety-four-hundred-foot Mount Stuart and the Stuart Range, the largest mass of exposed granite in North America. But from Elk Heights or even farther west, from Indian John Hill, where you see snowcapped mountains rise dramatically behind the town of Cle Elum, you can't tell that Cle Elum and neighboring Roslyn used to be coal towns, or that the Yakima River, which first meets the freeway near Cle Elum, has been funneling salmon to Columbia River fishermen for millennia.

The Yakima rises north of Lake Keechelus, flowing out of the lake where it is controlled by a Bureau of Reclamation dam. It has been used since the late nineteenth century to irrigate fields in the Yakima Valley, which produces apples, mint, hops, wine grapes, and some seventy other crops. For centuries before the Yakima was channeled into irrigation canals,

From Elk Heights you see the first dramatic view of Mount Stuart and the Stuart Range. Part of the North Cascades, the Stuart Range is the largest mass of exposed granite in North America.

Cle Elum, once a major coal-mining center, seeks to retain its identity and improve its economic base as local jobs and industries shift from natural resources to tourism and recreation. Near the town, Lakes Cle Elum and Kachess are major recreational attractions. The pressure of growth along Puget Sound is already making itself felt in Kittitas County towns east of the Cascade crest.

it produced fish that were caught by Native Americans with spears and dip nets on the Columbia River at The Dalles and Celilo Falls, and then dried, eaten, or traded with other tribes. Salmon bones found at the ancient Indian fishing and trading site at The Dalles are nearly eight thousand years old. Yakima River salmon were presumably some of the fish whose sheer numbers impressed Lewis and Clark in 1805. Some of the river's salmon still sustain a Yakima tribal fishery, and others are caught by commercial and sport fishermen in the lower Columbia.

In the late nineteenth and early twentieth centuries, miners from all over Europe and parts of Asia migrated as far as any salmon to the coal mines of Cle Elum and neighboring Roslyn. These small towns in the eastern Cascades became home to people from dozens of ethnic groups. The population of Roslyn, never more than four thousand, included Austrians, Belgians, Chinese, Croatians, Czechs, Dutch, English, Finns, Germans, Hungarians, Irish, Italians, Lithuanians, Montenegrins, Norwegians, Poles, Russians, Scots, Serbs, Slovenes, Swedes, Syrians, and Welsh. *Washington: A Guide to the Evergreen State*, first published in 1941 by the WPA Writers Project, reported that "many quaint Old-world traditions survive among the citizens. . . . A courtship custom among the Croats and Slavs decrees that, when a man wishes to propose, he must take a crowd of men friends to the girl's house and there, on bended knees, make his proposal. If he is rejected, he buys a keg of beer in which the common grief may be drowned; if he is accepted, his friends pay the wedding fees."

The Northwest's first significant group of African-Americans was originally brought to Roslyn in 1888 to work as strikebreakers in the mines. No one would hire black workers under other circumstances. The African-

Americans stayed after the strike, becoming part of the regular workforce and the community. The WPA guide noted that the town celebrated Emancipation Day every August 4.

Miners of all races and cultures lived constantly with the threat of dying underground in a cave-in or an explosion. One man survived the sinking of the *Lusitania* during World War I, then went back to Cle Elum and died in the mines. All the miners worked together and drank together, but each ethnic group lived in its own neighborhood and buried its dead in its own cemetery.

After the Great Depression, when oil increasingly replaced coal for heating and transportation fuel, the mines' days were numbered. The big coal companies pulled out first. Small independent miners hung on into the 1960s, but in 1963 people stopped mining coal in the Cascades. Tailings from the old mines still rise almost like natural hills behind downtown Roslyn and Cle Elum. But now Roslyn is known primarily for its role as a fictional Alaskan village in the television series "Northern Exposure"; when the television cameras are rolling, streets are closed off, and crowds of visitors stand on the sidewalks to watch the actors work.

In the late nineteenth century, immigrants came from all over Europe and parts of Asia to dig coal in Roslyn (*top left*). They all worked together in the mines, but each ethnic group had its own neighborhood and its own cemetery, like this one for Italian miners (*bottom left*). The last coal mines closed in 1963, and in the early 1990s Roslyn became famous as the fictional Cicely, Alaska, in the television series, "Northern Exposure." *Above:* When a series episode is being filmed, the town's streets are blocked off and tourists gather to watch the actors work.

Past the turnoffs to Roslyn and Cle Elum, I-90 climbs into the mountains. At Easton, just before the pass narrows and the grade steepens, you can turn off to find Iron Horse State Park. Today Easton is known mostly as the place where snow in Snoqualmie Pass forces westbound drivers to pull off the road and put on chains. Before World War II, though, Easton was a railroad fuel and water stop; Iron Horse park is split by the old Milwaukee Railroad route, now the John Wayne Pioneer Trail. Walk along the trail on any hot, sunny day, and you'll catch the smell of warmed pine. It's not a scent you'll find farther west, where you walk through the shade of hemlock and fir. The pine woods stop on this dry side of the Cascade crest. Before old-growth pines were logged and people started preventing—or trying to prevent—forest fires, native tribes used fire to clear away underbrush, and the woods were so open people could drive wagons among the trees.

Beyond Easton the road turns and climbs, emerging at Lake Keechelus, where it runs along the lakeshore, pinned at one point between the water and solid rock. In the 1870s and 1880s, when people drove livestock across the mountains to sell in Seattle, the swampy eastern shore of the undammed and narrower lake was a particularly troublesome spot. When Morris Jenkins, who moved to this area in 1929, got married in Idaho three years later, the elderly justice of the peace who married him said that he himself had driven cattle through the pass in the 1880s, and this had been the worst spot of all. Between the devil's club and the biting flies, the cattle were just about uncontrollable. Some took off into the woods. Years later, when Jenkins was surveying in that area, above Resort Creek, he found an old steer's skull, green with algae.

Even if you weren't driving cattle, the insects in the pass could be fierce. Dionis G. Reinig, who owned land near North Bend, recalled in 1966

Heading west toward Snoqualmie Pass, I-90 borders Lake Keechelus. Water stored here irrigates orchards, vineyards, and row crops in the Yakima Valley.

The ski areas at Snoqualmie Pass, only an hour's drive from Seattle, provide the largest night-skiing operation in the world. Many skiers drive there after work. These slopes and the cross-country trails nearby offer winter recreation to thousands of people each year.

that when crossing the pass around 1894, "the horses were almost driven wild by large deer flies that were about the size of horse flies and seemed to have hard shells on their backs. We cut huckleberry branches and fought them off. When the road was good enough to gallop our horses we could get away from them, but when we looked back we could see them coming. We would fight them again until we had another chance to out-run them."

Not everyone who crossed the pass could escape its torments with a burst of speed. Reinig wrote that "we saw many broken down wagons and dead horses and cattle by the side of the road. The man who collected tolls at the toll gate had several wagons that travelers had had to leave because some part had broken and they could go no further."

Opposite: After crossing Snoqualmie Pass and descending toward Seattle, I-90 passes the sharp peaks of McClellan Butte, a popular day hike for urbanites. The mountain is named for Civil War general George McClellan, who, as a young officer, tried and failed to find a route through the Cascades.

Today one is most likely to find abandoned wagons in the dead of winter, when the pass gets thirty-five feet of snow. Then, even though snowplows work around the clock, drivers expect to tune in their radios for road conditions and, very likely, pull over at a lighted roadside area to put chains on their cars. A lot of them also expect to stop at the summit and ski. After Gold Creek, the freeway passes the first of four ski areas. Snoqualmie is the only major American ski center located on an interstate highway. So close to the city that people can drive there after work, it has far and away the largest night-skiing operation in the world.

At the summit the road heads straight toward a mountain, veers left, and plunges down the western slope, curving around another mountain and, four miles later, crossing Denny Creek. Anyone who wonders what the old forest was like could do worse than take the Denny Creek exit and walk the nature trail named for turn-of-the-century Seattle photographer Asahel Curtis. The trail winds through perhaps the best example of Northwestern ancient forest that is this easy to reach. You start out being impressed by trees three and four feet in diameter but soon encounter much bigger trees. The great, saurian plates of old-growth Douglas fir bark don't look much like timeworn stone, but apart from that, the name "cathedral forest" seems perfectly accurate: as at Notre Dame or Chartres, the great columns lead the eye —and the spirit—up, always up, until they disappear in the dim light above. Lower down, like old stained glass, the foliage of saplings, back-lit by the sun, seems to glow with its own light.

Beside the trail you may find a five-foot log almost rotted into the earth. It takes hundreds of years to grow a tree that big; it takes hundreds more for the wood to rot. That tree may have, in Robert Frost's words, been smoldering with "the slow, smokeless burning of decay" since before the American Revolution.

If you go early in the year, the trail may be blocked by chest-high trunks of trees that fell in winter storms. A shattered cedar perfumes the air. The living trees, some probably five hundred years old, may inspire thoughts about the passage of time, the continuity of life, the brevity of human existence. The newly fallen trees invite you to contemplate the randomness of fate: they stood here for centuries, survived countless windstorms and thunderstorms, forest fires, and snows—why have they fallen now?

Up on the freeway, Denny Creek marks the start of a roughly fourteen-mile de facto elk-crossing zone. Like cougars, elk use the Cedar River watershed as a sanctuary. Probably six hundred of them live there. But the big animals don't stay put; they are often on the move. One is known to have wandered from the watershed to the slopes of Mount Adams, eighty miles south. Others wander into the nearby woods, where they are shot by hunters. Some—from the watershed or elsewhere—cross the freeway. Or they try to cross. They leap easily over the chain link fence. Some clear the fences on both sides. Others find that a vehicle moving at freeway speed—maybe a semi rolling west with a full load of alfalfa hay—is nothing that evolution has equipped them to avoid. The number of road kills along this stretch of highway suggests that elk often try to cross here. The presence of elk on both sides of the road suggests that a lot of them make it.

Below Denny Creek, the road heads for the sharp peak of McClellan

Butte, named for the Civil War general who, a decade before Abraham Lincoln stripped him of command for his reluctance to fight the Confederates, searched for a route through the Cascades. He showed a similar reluctance to tackle the snows of Snoqualmie Pass and never made it across.

Past McClellan Butte, the road crosses the dirt and gravel of Grouse Ridge—no granite by the roadside here—a low, flat-topped berm that spreads across the head of the Snoqualmie Valley. Grouse Ridge is a moraine left by the Vashon glacier, which covered the Puget Sound basin with three thousand feet of ice during the last big glaciation, fifteen thousand years ago. This is as far east as the glacier got.

From the old moraine, the road drops into the Puget Sound basin, the open land that the pioneers knew as Ranger's Prairie. To the left, a road leads past the east side of Rattlesnake Mountain, under gray stone cliffs, to the Cedar River watershed. There Rattlesnake Lake, formed after the Cedar River was impounded behind a city of Seattle dam, floods part of what used to be known as Rattlesnake Prairie. No one ever claimed that rattlesnakes lived there. According to one story, a soldier who had last slept east of the mountains opened his bedroll on the prairie and found a dead rattlesnake that had evidently crawled in the night before. According to a more widely accepted version, camas lilies originally grew all over the prairie, and when their seed pods dried, a wind would make them rattle like so many snakes in the grass.

Along the northern flank of Rattlesnake Mountain, you reach the turnoff for the towns of North Bend and Snoqualmie. Both are old logging and sawmill communities. The Weyerhaeuser Company has run mills in Snoqualmie since World War I, and the cedar staves for the original wooden

Mount Si rises behind North Bend's Mar-T Cafe, which appeared often in the popular television show "Twin Peaks." Tourists continue to visit the Mar-T regularly.

Steam rises from the Weyerhaeuser mill in Snoqualmie. The mill began to cut lumber in 1917, but because it was geared to cutting old-growth trees rather than smaller second- and third-growth logs, the original sawmill became obsolete. Today the mill dries and finishes lumber that has been cut elsewhere but remains a prominent part of the town and is the base for Weyerhaeuser's Cascade operations, including a 167,000-acre tree farm in the Snoqualmie Valley.

Opposite: The Snoqualmie Valley near Carnation remains a center of dairy farming. Some of the pastures were preserved when King County voters passed the Farmlands Preservation bond issue in 1979 and development rights to the land were purchased. Northwest residents have repeatedly shown that they believe deeply in the importance of preserving natural resources.

pipeline that carried water from the Cedar River to Seattle at the turn of the century were milled at North Bend. (A section of the old pipeline can be seen near the watershed administrative complex.) Both towns got some national notoriety—and still get some tourists—as the setting for the short-lived but much-discussed television series "Twin Peaks." Mount Si, Snoqualmie Falls, an old Weyerhaeuser sawmill, and North Bend's Mar-T Cafe were all visual staples of the show. People with cameras and foreign accents still look around the Mar-T.

The towns got more local notoriety in November 1990, when the Snoqualmie River poured over its banks and into the streets. Flooding was nothing new, but this was the worst flood on record. Water flowed into three hundred of Snoqualmie's five hundred houses and drove the police and city administration from city hall. People took shelter in the Snoqualmie Valley Hospital and the North Bend Elementary School. Great stacks of lumber from the Weyerhaeuser mill wound up half a mile downstream.

When the river isn't flooding, you can drive northwest to Snoqualmie Falls and then to Fall City, where the Raging River meets the Snoqualmie. Before there was an I-90, before a bridge crossed Lake Washington, the old road forked at Fall City, and drivers heading for Seattle could go either south of the lake through what was still the coal town of Renton, or north through Redmond. A driver who wanted to take the "short route" would cut off route 202 to Kirkland and take a ferry to Seattle's Madison Park. A modern driver can still take 202 through fallow fields and second-growth trees to Redmond, now a center of high-tech industry. When the old Sunset Highway was built, Redmond was a supply center for farms and lumber mills. "Excitement ran high in 1935," recalled the WPA's *Washington: A Guide to*

The old roads, their bridge rails softened by time and vegetation, have come to seem part of the landscape. A short distance from the edge of I-90, you can reach places where the sound of running water drowns out the sound of passing cars.

the Evergreen State, "when a black bear strayed into town, was treed, and, despite efforts of townspeople and police, sheriff and deputies, remained in the tree three days." Redmond may not offer that kind of excitement anymore, but it is the place where you can pick up the Sammamish Trail, walk or cycle to the Burke-Gilman Trail, and follow it all the way to Seattle.

You can also drive up the east side of the Snoqualmie Valley to Carnation. There, from a wooden suspension bridge over the Tolt River at MacDonald Park, much of the year you can look over brilliant green fields to the snowy Cascades or watch steelhead fishermen standing in the river, silhouetted like dark pilings against the glare of late-afternoon sun on the water. At Carnation Farms, started as a research dairy in 1910, there is a statue of a cow named Segis Pietertje Prospect, familiarly known as Possum Sweetheart, who in 1920 set a world record for the most milk produced by a cow in a single year. An admiring article in a London dairy publication referred to her as "the most wonderful cow in the world."

The town of Carnation used to be known as Tolt, but after the dairy set up shop there, it changed its name. The lower Snoqualmie Valley still contains several dozen dairy farms, some protected from urban development after 1979, when King County voters authorized a public bond issue to buy development rights. Snoqualmie Valley farms are unusually productive: Washington leads the nation in milk produced per cow—it's always number one or two—and King County farms are among the most productive in the state. The quality of feed available from eastern Washington is high—some of those semis piled high with alfalfa rolling west through Snoqualmie Pass are heading for the dairy farms—and the climate seldom gets hot or cold enough to stress the cows.

If you don't leave I-90 at North Bend and Snoqualmie, you soon reach the turnoff for State Route 18, which runs south along the Raging River between Rattlesnake and Tiger mountains, crosses the Cedar River watershed, and leads into the Green River Valley, which was once the Seattle area's richest farming region.

If you stay on I-90, you see a log yard on the right, marking the community of Preston. Originally, the sawmill that stood beyond the log yard *was* the town. Its steam whistle got people up in the morning. It also generated electricity for the town, first lighting the plant and the bosses' houses, later lighting the workers' homes, each protected from the neighbors' cows by its own picket fence. Virtually everyone worked there. The Preston mill was founded by a Swede, August Lovegren, and for decades men came directly from Sweden to work in it. Lovegren was a Baptist from the Varmland region. People said that if you were Swedish, you might have a job at the mill, but if you were a Swedish Baptist, you did have a job at the mill. The loggers were Swedes from Jamtland who were not Baptists; they lived in a separate neighborhood and, presumably because they danced and drank, were known as the "sinners." The church kept its records in Swedish. Up through World War II, business was conducted in Swedish. As late as World War II, *Washington: A Guide to the Evergreen State* described Preston as "a settlement bordering the millpond of the Preston Mill Company, whose plant quite overshadows the village." The mill closed in 1970, reopened under different ownership a few years later, and seemed to be succeeding by cutting lumber to the dimensions used in Japan. It burned down in 1989, though, and wasn't rebuilt. Preston found itself a mill town without a mill. One option was to attract industry, virtually any industry, to the old industrial land. Residents, many of whose families had lived in Preston for generations, decided they didn't want that; they wanted to preserve the character of their community. They asked King County to have the whole town declared a historic district and started a public process of deciding what kinds of development would be compatible with the town as it had always been. Today, the community's future is very much up in the air, but its preferences are clear.

Beyond Preston, at High Point, I-90 passes another old mill site, this one completely obliterated by time and the construction of the freeway. At the turn of the century, though, the High Point mill was a major employer— people commuted from Issaquah to work there—and a major source of cedar lumber and shingles.

Now High Point is conspicuous mainly for the line of cars parked along a frontage road just south of the freeway on any day of the week. People driving by sometimes wonder what the owners of all those cars are doing there. The answer is—hiking. High Point is a trailhead for a whole network of trails through the Tiger Mountain State Forest. It is the busiest trailhead in the state.

Past High Point, the road curves around Tiger Mountain and descends to Issaquah. Businesses, mobile homes, and warehouses crowd the freeway. Lake Sammamish is visible to the north. Hundreds of houses are sandwiched between the lake and the freeway. You have clearly entered the Seattle metropolitan area.

In that setting, the slope of Cougar Mountain, to the south, seems remarkably undeveloped. In a single thirty-minute walk from the edge of I-90, you can reach a little valley where the sound of running water drowns out the sound of passing cars, where cedars two and three feet across grow beside the stream, where you can spot a single, perfect white trillium in early spring, where you can climb above the stream and be startled by old-growth Douglas fir trunks arching toward sunlight from the slopes. Cougars are still seen now and then on Cougar Mountain, patches of old-growth timber survive along the northern precipice, and there are trails where civilization seems far away.

The slopes of Cougar Mountain are riddled with old mine tunnels. Coal production peaked there in 1907, but people kept mining for more than half a century afterward, up to 1963. Nearly three-quarters of a million tons of coal were shipped from Newcastle, on the mountain's west side, in the 1870s, and in the 1880s Newcastle and the nearby community of Coal Creek made up the second-largest population center in King County. Seattle itself was occasionally called "the Liverpool of the West."

Today people dig around the edges of Cougar to build foundations for houses and mini-malls. This area grew rapidly all through the mid- and late 1980s. You see evidence of that growth almost immediately when I-90 reaches Bellevue. Once known primarily for its farms and its annual strawberry festival, Bellevue became a classic post–World War II bedroom suburb. It has since become a real city, with its own employment center and high-rise skyline. High-tech office buildings line the freeway, and houses crowd together on the hills. The only sizable patch of trees visible from I-90 marks the campus of Bellevue Community College.

The road comes over the crest of a hill at Eastgate, providing a dramatic view of the Seattle skyline silhouetted against the Olympic Mountains. Then it crosses Mercer Slough, a wetland preserved by the city of Bellevue, hurdles a narrow strip of Lake Washington, bores through Mercer Island in a concrete trench and tunnel, and then spans the rest of the lake.

Stippled with white sails on a summer day, lapping against the roadway in a winter storm, Lake Washington is a textbook example of a body of water brought back from the dead. In the 1950s, algae feeding on treated sewage effluent multiplied wildly and died by the billions; decaying, they took up oxygen in the water, making the lake environment increasingly hostile to other forms of life, and fouled the lakefront with their stench. The people of the Seattle metropolitan area voted in 1958 to create Metro, a new organization that would handle all the region's sewage, and to pay for huge pipes and treatment plants that could keep sewage out of the lake. This was the first major commitment made by any urban population to fight pollution. It paid off. Between the early 1960s and the early 1980s, the transparency of the lake water increased sevenfold. "The biological response of the lake has been dramatic," writes Arthur R. Kruckeberg in *The Natural History of Puget Sound Country* (Univ. of Washington Press, 1991). Kruckeberg notes that the Lake Washington story has been "a challenging and yet realizable model for communities all over the world."

Salmon still use the lake, as do swimmers, wind-surfers, and boaters. The water serves as a front yard for lakefront houses and for both city and

The wetlands of Mercer Slough have been preserved by the city of Bellevue. This magnificent four-hundred-acre preserve is just off the freeway and serves as a natural gateway to this city of eighty-nine thousand residents.

I-90 has been recessed and covered where it crosses Mercer Island. That kind of construction is very expensive but minimizes the freeway's impact on a community. Parks and basketball courts will be constructed on the lids.

county parks, including the string of parks designed early in this century by the Olmsted brothers along the eastern edge of Seattle.

Once I-90 reaches that edge of the city, it plunges through another tunnel and dumps cars into the bleak warehouse and industrial area near the Seattle Kingdome. You drive off into a maze of featureless buildings, small, unpaved parking lots, and tiers of plastic seats stored behind chain link fence in the huge Kingdome parking lot. The nineteenth-century buildings of Pioneer Square stand nearby, though, as do the Goldrush National Historic Park—commemorating the days when Seattle was the main jumping-off point for the Klondike gold rush—and the downtown waterfront.

You can stand in Waterfront Park and see tall, orange cranes loading Asia-bound container ships, a factory trawler home from catching groundfish in Alaska, ferries carrying people back and forth across Puget Sound. The predecessor of Coleman Dock, where the ferries land, was headquarters for the Mosquito Fleet steamers that carried passengers and freight around the sound until World War II. Just a little south is the site of Yesler's Wharf (built in the mid-nineteenth century with rocks carried north as ballast on sailing ships from San Francisco), which helped make Seattle a major port. Nearby to the north, a plaque marks the spot where the steamer *City of Portland* landed with the "ton of gold" that inspired the Klondike gold rush.

From Waterfront Park you can also watch the sun set behind the Olympics. You saw the same profile of the Olympics from the top of Mount Si and from the freeway at Eastgate, but now you're seeing it from sea level. The sound, gouged by the same south-flowing glacier that dug the trenches of Lakes Washington and Sammamish, that left the moraine at Grouse Ridge, laps at the pilings below your feet. Your next stop may be for a caffè latte in the Pike Place Market or Pioneer Square, but your imagination can ride the salt water, as ships leaving Seattle have ridden it for more than a century, to Alaska or Hawaii or Asia.

A journey along the greenway ends in downtown Seattle on the shore of Puget Sound. Standing by the water, looking west to the Olympic Mountains, you're close to the nineteenth-century brick buildings of Pioneer Square—and to warehouses, parking lots, and a tangle of crowded streets.

This is a natural place for the journey to end. All the rain that falls on the west-facing slopes and foothills of the Cascades flows, in time, to Puget Sound. The coal mined in the nineteenth and early twentieth centuries and much of the lumber cut along the I-90 corridor wound up on the Seattle waterfront, too. For anyone who has driven west on the freeway from Issaquah or Roslyn—or Boston—Seattle is the end of the line.

The salt water forms a natural barrier that keeps the city from spreading west. No natural barrier keeps the city from spreading east to the high Cascades. And even the Cascades no longer keep people out of the urban economy: workers have started commuting across the mountains from Cle Elum. I-90 makes it possible. When traffic is light, the drive from Cle Elum to the businesses east of Lake Washington takes little more than an hour. The drive from Issaquah to downtown Seattle takes twenty minutes. From Issaquah to Bellevue, you barely have time to get your radio tuned in. However much people complain about traffic jams, this kind of easy transportation makes eastward growth inevitable; all else being equal, that growth will probably take the form of sprawl. There is no question that people and businesses will keep moving east along the freeway corridor. The question is whether or not the landscape and the existing communities will be changed beyond recognition. What will the trip from Cle Elum to Puget Sound feel like in ten years? What will it feel like in fifty?

The view over Elliott Bay probably won't change a great deal. But farther east the future of the views, the trails, the surviving evidence of the region's history, the network of habitat that enables large predators to reach the edge of the metropolis is still up for grabs.

MOUNTAINS TO SOUND MARCH 1990

JULY 4 THROUGH JULY 8, 1990

An 88-mile walk from Snoqualmie Pass to Puget Sound along the "Greenways" of the Interstate 90 corridor. Overnight camping at Rattlesnake Lake, Preston, Issaquah and Newcastle Beach Park.

End-to-end hikers must register with the Issaquah Alps Trails Club. Write: "Mountains to Sound March," c/o Issaquah Alps Trails Club, P.O. Box 351, Issaquah, WA 98027. 24-Hour Hotline: 328-0480. Applications for the full hike are available at King County libraries, King County Parks and Recreation offices, and outdoor equipment stores.

Free day hikes are scheduled all along the Mountains to Sound route from July 4 through 8. Day hike schedules are available at the same places as applications.

This poster was made possible in part by generous contributions from The Boeing Company; REI; High Mountain Rendezvous of Gilman Village in Issaquah; Perkins Coie, a law firm with offices in Seattle and Bellevue; King County Natural Resources and Parks Division and individual contributions from members of the Issaquah Alps Trails Club. © 1990 Issaquah Alps Trails Club

Chapter III

A Vision of the Greenway

On the sweltering Independence Day morning of 1990, eighty-five people worked their way down a steep bank in the western Cascades, gripping a knotted polypropylene rope strung from tree to tree. This was the first hard descent in an eighty-eight-mile hike, and Ted Thomsen of the Issaquah Alps Trails Club, which co-sponsored the hike, had rigged the rope—once used to tow gliders at the by-then-defunct Issaquah Skyport—for handholds on the way down. The people clinging to Thomsen's rope had started that morning at Snoqualmie Pass on the Pacific Crest Trail, and they were climbing down to a gravel roadbed abandoned by the Milwaukee Railroad. They had just started a five-day Mountains to Sound March that would lead them to Seattle's Waterfront Park. The march was being held to dramatize the idea of a Mountains to Sound Greenway, a corridor of linked trails, wildlife habitat, and natural views from the crest of the mountains to salt water.

That July Fourth morning was a rough beginning. Jack Hornung, also of the Issaquah Alps Trails Club, who dreamed up and organized the march, wrote later that "we got off on the wrong foot. . . . The weather was hot, the gravelly trail horrible on the feet. By the end of the day, with a little snow added for effect, [Seattle Opera director] Speight Jenkins could have cast our marchers in his operatic production of *War and Peace* as Napoleon's wounded troops on the way back from Moscow."

Hornung, who had moved to Seattle from Philadelphia, worried that the region was in imminent danger of losing the qualities that had attracted him, that it would "lose its very essence." He had a sense of how quickly a place's character could change; in the east, older hiking companions had pointed out ugly, developed valleys that they remembered as open and beautiful. Hornung also felt that it was possible to preserve land even in heavily urban areas. He had lived near Philadelphia's river-corridor parks, which provide strips of land wild enough for deer and foxes in the heart of the nation's fourth-most-populous metropolitan area. And he was familiar

The 1990 Mountains to Sound March promoted the idea of a greenway—a corridor of linked trails, wildlife habitat, and natural views from the crest of the mountains to Puget Sound. Marchers hiked eighty-eight miles, from Snoqualmie Pass to Elliott Bay, in five days.

Nearly one hundred hikers completed the 1990 Mountains to Sound March. They began on the Pacific Crest Trail near Snoqualmie Pass. Later the marchers camped beside Rattlesnake Lake.

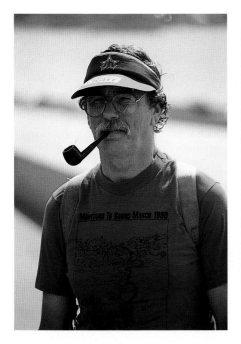 

Two of the leaders of the Mountains to Sound March: Jack Hornung (*left*) moved to Seattle from Philadelphia, where he saw how quickly a place's character could change, and was one of the first to advocate a Mountains to Sound Greenway. Ted Thomsen (*right*), a member of the Issaquah Alps Trails Club, played a large role in organizing the Mountains to Sound Greenway Trust and serves as secretary of its board.

with the writings of the pioneer planner Benton McKaye, who in the 1920s had conceived the Appalachian Trail, which runs two thousand miles along the eastern mountains from Maine to Georgia. McKaye had thought not simply of a trail but of an "Appalachian Empire," a strip of farms and undeveloped land that would serve as a refuge for people from the eastern cities and a barrier to halt the sprawl of city population along the nation's new motor roads.

In 1989, when Hornung was asked on short notice to address the Washington Wildlife and Recreation Coalition, he talked about creating a greenway along the I-90 corridor. Asked to show the group a written proposal, he stayed up late one night and, aided by a few friends from the Issaquah Alps Trails Club, put together "'Wilderness on the Metro': A Proposed Mid–King County Natural and Recreational Corridor for Man and Beast," which became known as "the green book."

The green book started by quoting Seattle-area author and environmentalist Harvey Manning. "The saving of the green spirit of Puget Sound City would be a model for elsewhere," Manning said. "The green and pleasant land is becoming gray, garish and noisy, indistinguishable from every fast food platter of hash spewed out by the developer's assembly line. While curing other ailments, Puget Sound City must stir itself to establish a refuge within, a place to breathe deep and clean, to feel and think green peace, to recreate."

The green book explained that "building on work that has been underway for the last two decades, we propose an expanded, interlinked, large scale, reclaimed wilderness corridor which would connect the County's western watery urbanized areas to its eastern mountains, thereby creating a kind of 'Central Park' for rapidly urbanizing King County." The book went on to define the outlines of what was then the greenway idea and announced that "in 1990, the Issaquah Alps Trails Club will organize a Mountains-to-Sound hiking event. . . . Taking our cue from a Mountaineers-sponsored hike of some years back, we will hike from Snoqualmie Pass to West Point, hopefully dramatizing the Corridor Concept—Wilderness on the Metro." (Metro, formed originally to handle the sewage that was polluting Lake Washington, had been managing King County's transit system for years.)

The idea of the march and the call for a greenway were all Hornung's, but ideas about a scenic route, a network of trails, a string of parks between the mountains and Puget Sound had been evolving for years. In 1903 the Olmsted brothers, whose father, Frederick Law Olmsted, had planned Manhattan's Central Park, Brooklyn's Prospect Park, and other landmarks, were brought to Seattle to design a system of parks and boulevards for the city. Their complete plan was never carried out, but enough of it was followed to give the city a chain of parks along Lake Washington connected by Lake Washington Boulevard. Charles E. Little suggests in *Greenways for America* (Johns Hopkins Univ. Press, 1990) that Frederick Law Olmsted's belief in linking parks together with green travel corridors makes him the father of the greenway idea. "The tracks of the great park-maker, Frederick Law Olmsted, are all over the modern greenway movement," Little writes. "Arguably, if any single person 'invented' the idea of greenways, it was he." Certainly, the string of parks along Lake Washington can be considered a kind of urban greenway; it has the connectedness, on a smaller scale and in a different setting, of the Mountains to Sound project.

King County park planners had envisioned a sound-to-mountains route in the early 1970s. In 1975 the county printed brochures that advocated linking existing trails north of Lake Washington, down the Snoqualmie Valley, and north of I-90 all the way to Snoqualmie Pass. Much of the route followed abandoned railroad lines, and the proposal was largely for converting "rails to trails." A King County planning employee named Stan Unger thought it would be fun to actually walk the proposed route, and in the rainy August of 1975, Unger spent five days hiking from Discovery Park to the pass. He walked railroad tracks through Seattle, followed the Tolt Pipeline Trail to the Snoqualmie Valley, hiked another abandoned railroad line— acquired but not yet developed by King County—up the valley to Snoqualmie Falls. Beyond North Bend Unger took logging roads north of I-90 into the mountains (trains still ran on the tracks south of the freeway, and he never imagined that the route that they ran over would become a trail), then followed hiking trails into what is now the Alpine Lakes Wilderness. (In 1990 Unger—by then a member of the Issaquah Alps Trails Club—worked with another club member, Ralph Owen, to find and in some places build a route for the Mountains to Sound March.)

Harvey Manning and other founders of the Trails Club had used the phrase "Wilderness on the Metro" in the mid-1970s when they started working to save trails and wild land on Cougar, Squak, and Tiger mountains. An early member of the group, Buzz Moore, who sat on the Metro Council, organized a bus ride from Seattle Center to Tiger Mountain that culminated in a hike up West Tiger and called it "Wilderness on the Metro 210."

When the Olmsted parks were just being built, Seattle city engineer Virgil Bogue suggested going beyond the city to create an ambitious network of parks and scenic roads radiating out in all directions. Bogue's plan included roads up the Cedar River and the middle fork of the Snoqualmie and a commitment by the city to "preserve . . . in primeval glory" the forests of the Cedar River watershed.

In more recent times, the Issaquah Alps Trails Club proposed an Issaquah Alps National Urban Recreation Area. A 1980 progress report on the Forward Thrust bonds that bought 4,776 acres of parks and open space in King County noted that some trails bought or developed with the bond money "form the first links for a Sound-to-mountain[s] trail running from Puget Sound to the Snoqualmie Summit."

Jack Hornung readily acknowledges that he was building on other people's work. "I saw the Alps as a wonderful thing," he says. "Why not extend it to the Cascades and to the city?"

A march seemed a natural way to call attention to the idea. Hornung had participated in civil rights marches during the 1960s and had earlier conceived the Issaquah Alps Grand Traverse, on which hikers covered Cougar, Squak, and Tiger mountains in one day. He and Tom Wood spent literally months of time organizing the Mountains to Sound March, working out the details, getting approval from many different government agencies, buying the insurance that public agencies required. There was, he recalls, "a mountain of minutiae."

But the march worked. It got press coverage and started people thinking and making plans. "I think it got the ball rolling and brought into focus the concept that had been brewing," Ted Thomsen says. "The march, I think, sort of pulled the trigger on the latent idea."

By 1990 western Washington wasn't the only place in which people were talking about greenways of one kind or another. But nowhere else did the idea embrace cougar habitat and old-growth Douglas firs, a range of altitude from mountain peaks to salt water, a range of density from wilderness to urban downtown. In few places has the idea embraced so much real estate. Still, by the time those eighty-five marchers set out from Snoqualmie Pass heading for Puget Sound, the idea of a greenway had been applied to a wide range of projects: creating foot or bicycle paths along old railroad rights-of-way or canal towpaths, like the Illinois & Michigan Canal National Heritage Corridor; preserving farms and undeveloped land along rivers, as in Oregon's Willamette Valley Greenway; preserving networks of open land along the ridges above urbanized valleys, as in northern California's Mid-Peninsula Regional Open Space District; preserving a combination of open space and historic sites, as in Pennsylvania's Lackawanna Valley Heritage Park. In 1987 the President's Commission on Americans Outdoors, appointed by Ronald Reagan, recommended setting up "a network of greenways across America." The idea had entered the mainstream.

In western Washington the march was followed in little more than a year by formation of the Mountains to Sound Greenway Trust. Regional officers of the Trust for Public Land (TPL), a non-profit organization that preserves open space in and around cities, played a key part in setting up the new group. TPL took the idea of a greenway and worked out the specifics needed to create an organization and a campaign. It suggested setting up the Greenway Trust and donated its own staff and office space so that the greenway campaign could start right away. TPL paid its associate regional man-

The Greenway Trust organized a Technical Advisory Committee to review, analyze, and offer advice on the complex patterns of land use, recreation, and cultural resources in the greenway corridor. A lot of the land that would form the greenway is already preserved. The challenge is to create a network, to link isolated areas together and prevent the sprawl that too often follows interstate highways.

One goal of the greenway is to preserve wildlife corridors. Many animals, such as these elk, travel long distances, crossing legal boundaries and ignoring fences. The animals need safe ways to cross the freeway and other main roads. They also need connections between habitat areas so that populations don't become isolated.

ager, Donna McBain, to serve as the Greenway Trust's executive director. Its regional manager, Craig Lee, joined the greenway board.

The chairman of the Greenway Trust was Jim Ellis, who had been honorary co-chairman of the Mountains to Sound March. Earlier Ellis had led the Forward Thrust campaigns and the campaign for a farmlands initiative that bought development rights to 12,568 acres of King County farms. He already had a strong personal attachment to part of the greenway: he had spent some memorable summers in his late teens in Preston when it was still very much a Swedish mill town. He still owned a log cabin he and a brother had built there beside the Raging River. Ellis broadened the greenway goals both conceptually and geographically.

So did other people who subsequently joined the greenway board. When Ellis and former state Commissioner of Public Lands Brian Boyle—the march's other co-chairman—assembled a board of directors, they cast their net as widely as they could. They wanted to be sure a full range of interests and opinions was represented inside the group. The board drew in representatives of local governments, state and federal agencies, corporations, and citizen groups that owned, managed, or had an interest in the fate of land within the greenway corridor. When these diverse board members thought about the greenway, they tended to emphasize different things. One focused primarily on trails, while another wanted to be sure commercial forestry survived. Some thought in terms of building regional consensus, while others emphasized the need to save specific parcels of land close to the road. After representatives from Kittitas County were included, a decision was made to carry the greenway not only beyond Snoqualmie Pass but beyond Cle Elum, where the route would start at the eastern approach to the Cascades. The greenway corridor now embraces both the eastern slopes and the dramatic westward views of the mountains. It also takes in areas east of Snoqualmie Pass that have already felt the development pressure spreading inland along I-90. There have been no fundamental changes. The details of the project have evolved, but the guiding vision has remained the same: creating pathways from the mountains to and through the city; preserving the irreplacable.

The basics are obvious: standing by salt water and looking up at snowcapped mountains, standing in the mountains and looking down at the sound, walking through big Douglas firs an hour or less from downtown Seattle are all experiences that have been a critical part of living here. They are a lot of what has made living here unique. The development that will inevitably follow the I-90 corridor from west to east threatens to leave the wild areas fragmented and isolated and to forever separate the Cascade Range from Puget Sound.

That doesn't have to happen. The transportation corridor itself can be used to link the mountains and sound aesthetically, biologically, and experientially. The greenway would use it in just that way.

The greenway idea has four major elements:

- **Preserve views along the freeway from the current eastern boundary of urban sprawl all the way through Snoqualmie Pass.** Today people can drive between Issaquah and Cle Elum through hills covered with trees; they look at the woods, not at houses or malls or mini–storage warehouses. They should still be able to do this ten, fifty, or one hundred years from now. Because an estimated fifteen million people a year make the drive, this is a matter of some social significance.

  However many trees are saved, some development will happen in places that are visible from I-90. Some tacky structures already crowd the road. To preserve the view, existing development

The state Department of Transportation had the foresight to construct a pedestrian and bike path on the I-90 bridge between Mercer Island and Seattle. Paths like this make it possible to link more rural, wilder areas to the city. Hikers or bikers may someday be able to start from their backyards in Seattle and follow a network of trails across Snoqualmie Pass to Elk Heights in eastern Washington.

As you drive west from Easton, the slopes on both sides of the freeway are green. The Greenway Trust wants to keep them that way by retaining forest and farms along the I-90 corridor.

Small communities along the greenway can maintain their distinct characters while their economies grow.
Buildings can be set back from the
freeway, and plantings and existing
forest can soften or hide their visual
impact. These artist renderings of
the area near Preston show how
development can blend with the
landscape, not overpower it.

along the highway should be screened, and new developments should use design and buffering to reduce their visual impact.

- **Preserve natural areas that are vital to the survival of wildlife.** These areas should be linked by corridors along which animals can and will safely pass. This will keep wildlife populations from being isolated, increasing their chances of survival. Avoiding the fragmentation of habitat has become a nationwide environmental goal.

- **Separate urban areas from each other.** Sprawl, which no one claims to like, homogenizes the landscape; one area melts into another until no recognizable places are left. Although no one claims to want the unrestricted growth for which Southern California is notorious, the patterns of Southern California are being repeated all over the United States. They can be repeated here, and if we rely only on traditional land-use regulation, they will be. Zoning by itself has proven a frail barrier against that kind of development. Permanent corridors of undeveloped land would form much longer-lasting barriers. They would interrupt the flow of development just as cleared firebreaks stop the spread of wildfire. They would create edges, clear outlines. Within those outlines, historically distinct areas would keep their boundaries and their characters.

- **Provide more opportunities for recreation and other human uses.** The greenway would make it possible for people to go from the mountains to the sound on foot. It would also make more trails, natural areas, and historic sites accessible to people who use public transportation.

Although the emphasis is on natural areas and outdoor recreation, nature isn't the whole story. The point is to preserve a regional heritage that includes places people have lived and things people have done in the woods and mountains for generations. Areas of historical significance will not only be preserved; they'll be explained by signs and displays and be made accessible to people traveling by foot, bicycle, car, or bus. Recognition of the area's history—logging, mining, and railroad building; centuries of travel and trade—can give current events and experiences added resonance.

A lot of the elements are already in place. The key is linking them together. From Cle Elum west through Snoqualmie Pass the corridor is relatively narrow and well defined. West of the pass it fans out, encompassing both forks of the old Sunset Highway to the northern and southern ends of Lake Washington and the current State Route 18, which angles south between Rattlesnake and Tiger mountains almost to Tacoma. Farther west the area is more built up, so it will be necessary to stitch together what in some cases are very small tracts or narrow corridors already surrounded by urban development. In some places hiking or cycling routes will have to be designated along city streets.

No one will come up with enough money to simply buy outright all the land that should be preserved or even the development rights to that land. (Buying just the 130,000 acres of commercial forest in the greenway corridor would cost an estimated one-quarter to one-half *billion* dollars.)

Therefore, two things will be essential: land swaps and the permanent preservation of what is now commercial forest. And preserving the forest will require two more things: making sure it remains profitable to grow and harvest trees and resolving questions about the ways trees are harvested. It may, for example, be a good idea to lengthen rotations, leaving more time between planting and harvesting. Clearcutting narrow swaths may be better than clearcutting square patches. Or it may be a good idea to practice "new forestry" and not clearcut at all. The Forest Service, the state Department of Natural Resources, and the forest-products industry are all experimenting with new methods in the greenway corridor.

The Greenway Trust's goal isn't to stop all growth. The tide of growth is coming in. No one wants to stand there like King Canute and order it out. Some natural areas and trails are already protected. Whatever happens, they will survive as islands in the urban sea. The idea is not only to create more islands but to link new and existing islands together so that people and wildlife can move among them instead of being isolated in the urban tide. The goal is, in fact, to make them something other than islands. And it is to create continuous visual corridors so that—to carry the metaphor further—someone traveling through the urban sea can continue to look at the land and can remain aware of the natural features and historical patterns that give this place its distinct character.

Opposite: Many people's nightmare for what could happen to the greenway corridor is the kind of rapid, unplanned, landscape-altering development that took place in Southern California. These two photographs, taken from near the same spot less than three decades apart, show the alarming transformation of California citrus groves to houses and industry.

Chapter IV

A Path Has Always Crossed These Mountains

The trail leads straight uphill. In some places it is faint and hard to follow through the massive alpine and silver firs. It could be a game trail or an illusion. In other places it is worn knee-deep through bunchgrass on the forest floor. Hiking trails and logging roads wind all through these mountains, but they aren't worn into the earth as this is. These channels through the forest tuft are like remnants of the old Oregon Trail, where you can still see ruts made by thousands of wagon wheels rolling west. But this trail is older than those wagon ruts in Oregon, and it was worn not by wheels but by feet, generations and centuries of feet. It is part of an ancient Indian route across the Cascades. More than half a century after he first trapped in these woods near Lake Keechelus, even though road-building and clearcuts have transformed the landscape and obliterated most of the old foot-worn tread, Morris Jenkins can still find two segments of the old Indian thoroughfare. "It's a trail," he says, "that'll never disappear."

When Jenkins arrived at Snoqualmie Pass in 1929, "it was all beautiful timber along the highway: tall and huge trunks. It's hard to realize today what the forest was like." Fires and avalanches had mowed down parts of the forest, so he found trees in all stages of growth, but among the big trees, "sometimes, it was hard to see the sun." The woods were still full of animals. "You could see them and you could hear them. The woods would be a continuous din: the woodpeckers and the squirrels barking and birds making sounds." In winter, "there were tracks everywhere: snowshoe rabbits and bobcats, squirrels, mice, bird tracks—everything."

Jenkins also remembers that "there were people all through the woods in those days." Traffic on the gravel road through Snoqualmie Pass was light, and weekends didn't bring thousands of city people to the ski slopes or hiking trails, but the woods themselves were full of people trapping, prospecting, trying to make a living from the land.

Morris Jenkins, who first trapped in the woods east of Snoqualmie Pass in 1929 and has known them intimately ever since, can still find segments of the old Indian trail across the Cascades.

Faint in some places and worn knee-deep in others, the Indian trail over Snoqualmie Pass leads straight uphill.

The trappers worked mainly in the winter. In the summer they occasionally trapped beavers whose dams were causing floods, but that was all. They didn't own the land on which they worked and lived, but each trapper had his own territory, everyone knew where it was, and no one infringed on it. Territories were even bought and sold. Poaching on another trapper's turf was a serious offense. In 1929 Jack Clark sold a trapline to Billy Clark (who was no relation). Billy subsequently accused Jack of robbing the traps. Jack got his rifle and Billy went for his own. The two men hid behind trees and blazed away at each other. Finally Billy wounded Jack. Then he put him on a homemade toboggan and pulled him through the snow to medical help.

Trappers and prospectors knew the woods intimately, and that meant they knew the old Indian trails. The Indian trails were still intact then, Jenkins says; in fact, they were more conspicuous than most Forest Service trails. Patrolling for the Forest Service in 1931, watching for fires and marking section lines, Jenkins often used one old Indian trail as a shortcut through the woods. On a long day, taking it was sometimes the only way he could get back home before dark.

In a region that European civilization first touched so recently, a region in which the native cultures, building with wood, left so little sign, these trail remnants are historical artifacts of rare age and value. They may be largely unknown and unprotected, but they are the real thing: man-made and ancient, they open a significant window onto regional culture.

Before settlers arrived in the 1850s, before Lewis and Clark explored the Northwest in 1805 or George Vancouver sailed along the coast in 1792, the trails were here. Before concrete highways, steel rails, or even dirt wagon roads crossed the mountains, they led people through the passes. The first non-Indian settlers and explorers didn't find a trackless wilderness. Tracks were already worn into the earth; the explorers just didn't know where to look. They realized, though, that the Indians did, and when George McClellan and other nineteeth-century Americans set out to "find" a way across the Cascades, they asked the Indians how to go. Indians ultimately guided Lieutenant Abiel Tinkham in the winter of early 1854 when he made the first recorded crossing of the mountains from Lake Keechelus through Yakima Pass, which lies just south of Snoqualmie Pass, down the Cedar River drainage, and into the Snoqualmie Valley. Tinkham probably followed the steep route still visible on the forest floor as he climbed to the ridgeline above Lake Keechelus. Four years later, when Major J. H. H. Van Bokkelen of the Washington Territorial Volunteers made the first government-backed crossing of Snoqualmie Pass itself, he followed an Indian trail to the summit.

No one knows how long ago tribes from both sides of the mountains started using these trails. The Snoqualmie Indians, who inhabited the valley and prairie below and above Snoqualmie Falls, traded smoked salmon and products of the coast to the Yakimas on the east side for roots and sun-dried salmon from the inland plateau. Every few years native people from both sides of the mountains gathered near the trail in the Kittitas Valley to trade, confer, and socialize. What McClellan and Tinkham saw as unbroken wilderness was in fact a major trade route. This situation wasn't unusual.

Gary Snyder observes in *The Practice of the Wild* (North Point, 1990) that when Europeans first arrived on this continent, "North America was all populated." All over the world, he writes, "there has been no wilderness without some kind of human presence for several hundred thousand years. Nature is not a place to visit, it is home—and within that home territory there are more familiar and less familiar places. Often there are areas that are difficult and remote, but all are known and even named." When white settlers reached the approaches to Snoqualmie Pass, the path through the mountains wasn't simply known, it was managed; the trail was controlled by a Snoqualmie chief, Pat Kanim, who lived below the falls and stationed guards all along the route.

People and merchandise moved both ways. Inevitably the constant contact between people from opposite sides of the mountains had cultural effects. The Snoqualmies who lived above the falls, around what is now North Bend, spoke differently from their relatives downstream. Of course, they inhabited different environments: below, people lived in a dark forest, caught salmon and sea-run trout in the Snoqualmie River, and used it and other rivers as travel corridors; above, there were no seagoing fish, and the more open country made it easier to travel overland. But environmental differences probably don't explain the variations in language. Presumably, says Seattle Pacific University anthropologist Ken Tollefson, the Snoqualmies above the falls talked differently because, being closer to the pass, they intermarried more with Yakimas, and their speech had more foreign influence.

By the time of the brief war between Indians and whites in 1855 and 1856, settlers were well aware that eastern tribes used the pass to travel west. When the war broke out, Washington militiamen commanded by Van Bokkelen built four forts—Tilton, a mile below Snoqualmie Falls; Alden, on the current site of Meadowbrook Farm; Smalley, on the current site of Tollgate Farm; and Patterson, near present-day Fall City. There was still no road, and Van Bokkelen wrote that "in all our movements we have gone through an entirely wild country." But he knew that "wild" didn't mean untraveled. He and his men were building the forts to keep eastern warriors from reaching Seattle and the settlements nearby.

White travelers and their goods started flowing over the ancient trail in the 1850s. Men heading for mining areas in eastern Washington walked across, and some led horses laden with up to 250 pounds of supplies.

But there was still no road on which to get a wheeled vehicle across. McClellan and Tinkham, who arrived just before the Indian war, were looking for a railroad route, but rails to Puget Sound lay more than two decades in the future, and the first routes didn't go through Snoqualmie Pass; in fact, more than half a century went by before anyone laid rails through the pass. Seattle boosters, working in a city connected to other settlements around Puget Sound and to the booming market of San Francisco only by water, hoped desperately for a land route to the east. They really wanted a railroad, but any way out of their isolation seemed a major step toward the growth and prosperity that virtually everyone wanted.

In 1865 a group of men from Seattle went up to the pass to survey the land for a wagon road. Seattle citizens raised $2,500 to begin construction. That summer William Perkins and a crew of twenty men set up camp at North Bend and started building a road east to the summit. It didn't take long for wagons to start rolling over the new road; the first caravan crossed from the east while Perkins and his men were still working their way toward the summit from the west.

Not all the traffic consisted of westbound wagons or eastbound miners. In the spring of 1869, cattle were first driven over the pass from Kittitas County. Soon so many cattle and sheep were making the trip that farmers on Ranger's Prairie, on the western side, went into the business of fattening them up on hay and rutabagas before they were driven on to Seattle. But long before they reached Ranger's Prairie, both livestock and wagons had to somehow make their way around Lake Keechelus, east of the summit. At the end of a dry summer they could use the exposed lake shore. The rest of the time people drove their animals over the slope above the lake or made rafts and floated them across.

In the fall of 1869, writes Clarence Bagley in his *History of King County, Washington* (S. J. Clarke, 1929), when M. S. Booth was returning from the Yakima Valley with 130 beef cattle, he found a group of immigrants with three wagons by the lake. "The horses had played out," Bagley writes, "several members of the party were sick, and Mr. Booth, upon his arrival in

For early settlers or ranchers herding livestock across the mountains, getting past Lake Keechelus was one of the hardest parts of the journey. Animals had to be driven over the slope above the lake or floated across on rafts. Some covered wagons crossed Lake Keechelus on a private ferry.

Seattle, gave it as his opinion that the party must be given assistance if it was to get through the pass before the winter rains set in and made the roads impassable. Seattle came to the rescue. . . . $100 was raised, and a man with a yoke of oxen was sent over the pass to [help] the stranded party which, a little later, was reported to have reached [Issaquah] in safety."

Winter rains were followed by winter snows, avalanches, landslides, and the falling of giant trees, so every spring the road had to be reopened. "Perhaps no other enterprise ever undertaken by our people has furnished so many disappointments as the building of the Snoqualmie Pass wagon road," wrote Bagley, who lived in Seattle while the building was going on. "Summer after summer, the fallen timber was removed from the road and winter after winter, the wind threw other forest giants down to again render the way impassable."

The road was largely useless for wagons throughout the 1870s and early 1880s, although pack trains and livestock moved regularly through the mountains. In 1883 the road was repaired and reopened as a toll road from the Taneum Creek bridge, southwest of Ellensburg, to Ranger's Prairie. The toll road was short-lived, however; in 1888 the Northern Pacific started running trains through Stampede Pass, south of Snoqualmie, to Tacoma, and the demand for a wagon route evaporated.

By that time the prairie west of the pass had become an agricultural center, and some people envisioned the nearby towns as centers of iron and coal mining. Farther west, sawmills were turning old-growth trees into lumber at mill towns all around Puget Sound. Sailing ships carried the lumber to San Francisco, Hawaii, and Asia. Seattle had become the supply center for the mill towns and also for the new territory of Alaska. People had started farming in the nearby river valleys, but overland travel was still difficult.

It had always been easier for both Indians and white settlers to travel on the rivers or the sound. When Seattle's first settlers found their supplies running low at the start of their first winter, Arthur A. Denny and David Boren paddled a canoe up the Duwamish and Black rivers to the Duwamish Indians' winter village on the Black, near the present city of Renton. They bought a canoe-load of potatoes and paddled back down. The round trip took them three days.

The difficulty of getting produce to the city didn't stop farmers from pushing up the valley toward Snoqualmie Pass. In 1868 the Norwegian

Construction and maintenance of a road over Snoqualmie Pass proved demanding. A wagon road was begun in 1865. Building the Sunset Highway across the Cascades in 1914 and 1915 was considered a great step forward. *Opposite:* Crossing the mountains by car could be quite an adventure, as drivers had to contend with mud, rocks, fallen trees, and running water. Sometimes, a horse team was better equipped for the journey than a car. *Top:* Until 1931 the highway was closed every winter and had to be cleared each spring. In 1934 it was finally paved. *Left:* Today, one of the highway's old bridges, almost lost beneath grass and moss and ferns, has become a latter-day ruin in the woods.

Wold brothers started growing hops on Ranger's Prairie, and the upper Snoqualmie Valley soon became a hop-growing center. At the beginning farmers brought in supplies and shipped crops along the Snoqualmie and Snohomish rivers. Boats could navigate the Snoqualmie as far as Fall City, where, in 1863, a wagon road had been cleared to Ranger's Prairie. In 1882 the valley's first homesteader, Jerry Borst—who had started out using the abandoned buildings of Fort Alden—sold much of his farm to the Hop Growers' Association, which quickly developed it into the largest hop ranch in the world. A wide variety of fruits and vegetables grew on the ranch, but hops were the main cash crop, and the hop vines stretched across the valley.

The hop industry didn't last long. Disease and a slump in the world market drove the hop ranch out of business. Instead of planting hops, most farmers in the Snoqualmie Valley were soon raising dairy cattle.

Even into the 1880s, when rails had reached Puget Sound from the Columbia River and the first brick buildings had gone up in downtown Seattle, it took a while for people to travel from the city to the country near Snoqualmie Pass. A reminiscence in the Seattle Public Library's collection describes a $2.50 trip to Snoqualmie in 1886: "I left Seattle by stage at 7 o'clock in the morning, going . . . from down town to Laurel Shade (Madison Park) on Lake Washington. There we took the little Steamer Bee, which conveyed a dozen of us to Houghton on the east side of Lake Washington. From Houghton we took another stage four miles west to the west end of [Lake Sammamish]. The passengers were immediately transferred to the waiting Steamer Economy, which in due time landed us at [the south end of the lake]. . . . The seventeen miles between there and the hop ranch was made on horseback." The narrator arrived by sundown, but it had been a long day.

Moving heavy objects over that route proved quite a challenge. In the 1860s and 1870s coal was discovered near Renton and Issaquah and at Newcastle, on the western slope of Cougar Mountain. In all three cases the trick was getting the coal to the Seattle waterfront, where it could be hauled on ships to San Francisco.

A Seattle gunsmith named C. B. Andrews found the Issaquah coal in the fall of 1862 and carried a sample out in an old flour sack. He and a Seattle blacksmith, William Perkins, became partners, and at the beginning of 1864 Perkins built a scow equipped with oars and a sail, hired a crew of Duwamish Indians, and poled his way up the Duwamish and Black rivers, sailed across Lake Washington, cut a path up the Sammamish Slough through logs and brush, and finally made it to the end of Lake Sammamish, where he loaded about five tons of coal. The round trip, with a layover at the head of Lake Sammamish, took him twenty days.

Hauling the coal mined at Newcastle posed less of a problem, but not much less. Coal was discovered there in 1863, on the bank of what has been known ever since as Coal Creek. When the first mine was developed, one load of coal was brought out in sacks, put onto a wagon, and hauled downhill to Lake Washington, where it was loaded onto a barge that ran aground in the Black River but finally made it all the way to Seattle. Starting in 1870 coal was taken by tramway to the lake, barged to Union Bay, taken by tram to Lake Union, barged to the south end of the lake, and taken on a final tram ride to the waterfront. The coal was handled eleven separate times along the way.

Coal at Renton was discovered in the 1850s, basically forgotten after the Indian war, and found again in 1873 when a Duwamish Indian named James Moses showed it to homesteader Erasmus Smithers. Smithers got backing from William Renton, who ran the huge sawmill at Port Blakely on Bainbridge Island. Coal from Renton also went down the Black and Duwamish rivers to salt water. In 1873 a locomotive was barged to Renton to haul coal from the mines to the Black River, and in 1875 a narrow-gauge railroad was built from the mines at Newcastle to the shore of Lake Washington. The railways saved some time and labor, but once the coal reached the water, it still took the long way around.

Local boosters still wanted a railroad to tie Seattle to the Midwest and ultimately the East. When news came that Tacoma had been selected as the western terminus of the Northern Pacific, the first transcontinental railroad to Puget Sound, citizens of Seattle started building their own railroad toward the Cascades. Optimistically named the Seattle and Walla Walla, the line never crossed the mountains or even reached them. (At around that time Walla Walla was the largest city in Washington. It had grown as an agricultural center and as an outfitting center for a gold rush on the Nez Perce reservation in Idaho.) The rails did reach the Renton mine in 1877 and the Newcastle mine in 1879, finally providing a nonstop route to salt water.

That still didn't help Issaquah get its coal to market. Daniel Gilman, who came west to run his brother's mines, had dreams of developing the coal and iron discovered by Arthur A. Denny in the Cascades. In 1885 Gilman wrote grandiosely from Seattle to a New York investment banker that "seventy-five miles back of this city in the Snoqualmie Pass is . . . a quantity of iron ore and white marble sufficient to supply the world." The iron never supplied anyone, although it inspired a brief boom in Kirkland, where Peter Kirk planned to build a big steel mill. Kirk actually put up a foundry and some smaller buildings and dug pits for two blast furnaces before his scheme collapsed. Bagley refers to "the great dream edifice reared at Kirkland by Peter Kirk." In 1888, however, Gilman completed the Seattle, Lake Shore and Eastern Railroad around the north end of Lake Washington, and Issaquah's coal was taken to market.

During the 1880s logging railroads were built into the woods around Puget Sound so that ox teams and gravity would no longer be the only forces that could move big logs to salt water. The Northern Pacific started building branch lines, too. Rails laid toward Snoqualmie Pass from the west opened the woods beyond Lake Sammamish to logging. And when the Northern Pacific laid tracks along the eastern Cascades in the 1880s, people started mining coal at Roslyn and Cle Elum in a big way. A subsidiary of the railroad company ran the mines in Roslyn, and Roslyn itself was a company town.

A second transcontinental railroad, the Great Northern, was completed to Seattle in 1893, still not using Snoqualmie Pass. A depression struck the country in 1893, and not much else was built or started in western Washington until it ended in 1897. Then the discovery of gold in the Klondike made Seattle a major port of embarkation, and a national wave of industrial expansion sent ripples through the area.

Coal mining was a big part of early economies of towns on both sides of the Cascades. The mines at Newcastle, on the western slope of Cougar Mountain, were still going strong in the late 1890s. Mine entrances and coal bunkers stood close to the town. The last mine closed in the early 1960s.

In important respects the region was taking its first steps into the twentieth century. In 1898 the Snoqualmie Falls Power Company started building an electric generating plant at Snoqualmie Falls, tunneling into solid rock for the original powerhouse. Power from the falls was sold in Seattle and Tacoma the next year. The generating plant at Snoqualmie was the first major hydroelectric project in Washington.

The growing city of Seattle started thinking about the Cedar River as a source of drinking water. Looking far beyond its needs at the time, the city bought large portions of its current Cedar River watershed and built a dam at Cedar Falls. In 1901 wooden pipe started carrying Cedar River water to Seattle. Four years later the city began using the Cedar River to power the first municipally owned generating plant in the United States. Water and electricity would flow from the mountains to the sound for the next century.

In 1899 the state legislature and the governments of King and Kittitas counties decided to repair the old wagon road over Snoqualmie Pass. It had been upstaged by the railroads and had fallen into disrepair, but it had never been abandoned. In fact, when David Denny started repair work—building bridges and blasting away boulders—in the summer of 1899, he reported that he put down nearly one thousand feet of corduroy on "a long piece of road where the mud was very deep and getting deeper by the constant travel." Denny "kept tally while on the road and found that from the time travel commenced until I closed work 94 wagons and carriages had passed over the road, 1,148 horses had crossed the mountains, and the travel has continued unabated up to the present time, so that nearly two hundred wagons have crossed. People come in their covered wagons from Michigan and many points east. I estimate fully 19/20 of those crossing come to make homes in the Puget Sound valley."

Summit of the Cascades Snoqualmie Pass on C.M. & St.P. Ry. C.P. Harper 12-1 CleElum, Wash.

The economic good times that started in 1897 continued, by and large, for more than a decade. For lumber mills, in fact, the end of that decade looked to be more prosperous than the beginning; San Francisco was destroyed by earthquake and fire in 1906, and lumber from western Washington was used to rebuild the city.

The year 1909 was a watershed. The Milwaukee Railroad finally completed a line through Snoqualmie Pass, tying Seattle to the last transcontinental railroad built in the United States. The new rails made the pass a major thoroughfare for goods and travelers once again. They also made it readily accessible for the first time to hikers and berry pickers from the city. The Mountaineers built a lodge a mile-and-a-half walk from the Milwaukee's Rockdale station, which occupied what is now the western entrance of the railroad's abandoned tunnel.

The city of Seattle had done well for itself since the depression ended. It was ready, in 1909, to celebrate more than a decade of rapid growth and to try putting itself on the map in a way that would attract more prosperity. Seattle's coming out party was the Alaska-Yukon-Pacific Exposition, held on what is now the University of Washington campus.

Among the people drawn to Seattle by the A-Y-P, as it was called, were five cross-country auto racers who started in New York. Cars had first been driven over the pass in 1905, but the road was still crude. After the 1909 race was announced, Kittitas and King counties repaired the road in places so that the auto racers could get through. Even then it was rough going: drivers followed creek beds and railroad tracks part of the way, and two vehicles were simply carried over the mountains on railroad cars.

The seed of the idea that Snoqualmie Pass could be an automobile route was planted in the public mind, and in 1914 the state began building

Earlier railroads chose other routes across the Cascades. But when the Milwaukee Railroad completed a line through Snoqualmie Pass in 1909, the new rails made the pass a major thoroughfare for goods and travelers once again. Trains stopped at Snoqualmie Summit, and hikers, picnickers, and cross-country skiers went by train to the pass.

1365
Wilse

The Black River connected Lake Washington to the Duwamish River and was an important transportation corridor for moving coal and other products to the Seattle waterfront. When the Lake Washington Ship Canal opened in 1916, the lake level dropped nine feet and the Black River disappeared, a reminder of the fragile balance between nature and human enterprise.

the Sunset Highway over the pass. The road opened in 1915, and cars started crossing Snoqualmie Pass in increasing numbers. The Sunset Highway wouldn't be paved for decades. It was rutted and muddy, and the first drivers across it in spring might have to cut their way through fallen trees just as the first people to cross it each year in wagons did. In winter the road was totally blocked by snow. But people used it. Automobiles soon became commonplace in the pass.

New technology made its way into the woods, too. In 1916 the Weyerhaeuser Company started building a huge new lumber mill at Snoqualmie. The company had owned land and timber in the area since 1900, but this was its first mill. The mill would not only be large, it would be modern: instead of crude logging camps, loggers would sleep in steam-heated railroad cars; all the machinery in the mill would be powered by electricity, as would machinery in the surrounding woods. Men actually laid long cables through the trees to reach the logging operations. Once the close-in trees were cut and the lengths of the cables grew prohibitive, the company gave up on electric logging. But the sawmill was a success and became the core of the community. Weyerhaeuser built a company town with houses, a YMCA, and a "hotel" that served as a boarding house for single workers. Railroad tracks ran into the mill yard and a train station stood near the office.

The mill didn't actually start cutting lumber until 1917, the year the United States entered World War I. The war created a great demand for timber, and shipyards boomed along Puget Sound and the shores of Lake Washington, attracting workers from all over the West.

The shipyard boom didn't outlast the war, but other things changed for good. Around Puget Sound, automobiles and trucks were displacing the old steamers that had tied communities together for more than half a century. Just when water transportation was becoming less important, work was finally completed on the Lake Washington Ship Canal, which provided a direct route from Lake Washington to Lake Union and then to salt water. The canal opened in 1916, dropping the lake level nine feet and creating a lot of new land around the shores. At the north end of the lake the tracks of the Seattle, Lake Shore and Eastern no longer ran along the water. There was now a strip of land between the rails and the lake, and before long people built houses on it. To the west, new land became part of the Olmsteds' chain of lakefront parks.

To the south, lake water no longer flowed through the Black River to the Duwamish. The Black, so recently a major transportation link, simply ceased to exist. David Buerge has written that the Duwamish Indian Moses family "watched as the river's flow slowed, then stopped, and the river died. Joseph [Moses] recalled the event: 'That was quite a day for the white people at least. The waters just went down, down, until our landing and canoes stood dry and there was no Black River at all. There were pools, of course, and the struggling fish trapped in them. People came from miles around, laughing and hollering and stuffing the fish into gunny sacks.'"

To the north, the Sammamish Slough remained but was no longer deep enough for navigation. The idea that Lake Washington would become a great harbor proved a pipe dream, but the town of Houghton did become a shipbuilding center, and Bellevue served as the winter quarters for a fleet of small Alaskan whaling vessels.

Beyond the lake, local coal mines faced stiff competition. The rise of the internal combustion engine meant that petroleum was used more widely as a fuel. In addition, cheaper coal was being mined in the Rockies. As World War I receded into memory, the market for coal from Roslyn and Cle Elum, Renton and Newcastle, began to fade.

Inland, as more and more old-growth trees were cut, some of the smaller mills began to fade too, but the big mills at Snoqualmie, High Point, and Preston were still going strong. Workers commuted from Issaquah to both High Point and Preston. Most of the old-growth forest on Tiger Mountain was fed to the mills during the 1920s, and carloads of logs were shipped from Issaquah.

The road through Snoqualmie Pass was graveled in the 1920s. When Morris Jenkins arrived there in 1929, he worked on the road filling potholes with hand tools and wheelbarrows. The road was still very rough. Tires were crude, and the roadside was usually dotted with drivers fixing flats. It was

At first there were no ski lifts or rope tows at Snoqualmie Pass. These members of the Cle Elum Ski Club were on their own.

also dotted with resorts at which vacationers could spend a night or a week.

The highway was still closed every winter, but huge rotary snowplows mounted on locomotives kept the railroad open. People began traveling by rail to ski areas. The first ski area in the greenway corridor wasn't at the pass but at Cle Elum. In the 1920s crowds went there not to ski but to watch ski-jumping competitions on a hill behind the mines. Most people who actually skied went cross-country, and members of The Mountaineers used the club's lodge at Snoqualmie Pass as a base for cross-country tours. In the 1930s the Milwaukee Railroad created the Snoqualmie Ski Bowl, on the present site of Hyak, which displaced Cle Elum as a ski-jumping center. The Seattle Ski Club set up two jumping hills of its own at the pass. The Seattle Park Board got permission from the U.S. Forest Service to use another piece of land and got a Civilian Conservation Corps crew to clear a slope at Snoqualmie Summit. The Park Board ran its own ski area there for years. When political pressure forced it to sell the ski area, the board's permit went to a private company called Ski Lifts, Incorporated—the employer of Webb Moffat, whose family now operates all the ski areas at the pass.

On the eve of World War II, Roslyn and Cle Elum were still mining towns with distinct ethnic communities. Renton was still a mining town, too. Production had faltered since World War I, but plenty of residents could remember when the 150-foot-high slag heap at the Old Strain mine smoldered for years, keeping the city under a blanket of smoke. Gyppo miners still worked the coal veins at Newcastle. The mills at Snoqualmie, High Point, and Preston were still turning out lumber.

The communities just east of Lake Washington were still largely agricultural centers. Bellevue was known for its berry farms, Newport as a place to buy fruit and vegetables from roadside stands. Kirkland was the largest community on the eastern shore. But completion of the first floating bridge from Seattle to Mercer Island and Bellevue in 1940 changed the economic geography of the area. Bellevue became a center of trade and, gradually, of population. The routes north and south of the lake became byways.

World War II changed the economy and transportation patterns of the whole area. Renton became a Boeing town instead of a mining town. Trains stopped carrying skiers and vacationers to Snoqualmie Pass. The road

With the opening of a floating bridge across Lake Washington in 1940, for the first time drivers at Issaquah knew they could drive straight across Lake Washington to Seattle, instead of looping north or south around the lake. This far east, they found open land and no signs of the city.

through the pass had been kept open all winter starting in 1931; it had been paved in 1934. Now, even with rationed gasoline, automobiles became the main way for people to reach ski slopes and hiking trails. When rationing ended and people with army-surplus skis took to the mountains, cars remained the transportation of choice. When the Milwaukee Railroad's ski lodge burned down, it wasn't replaced.

The Seattle area boomed again during the war. Boeing mushroomed, but old industries and the communities that had grown up around them were no longer central to the regional economy. A lot of the changes were permanent.

Although old mills and mill towns survived the war—Weyerhaeuser still ran a company town at Snoqualmie, and dozens of men lived in the company hotel—most of the big trees were gone. Suburban housing started taking over fields on the east shore of Lake Washington. The number of automobiles exploded. Fuel oil was rapidly replacing coal for home heating, and the surviving mines were becoming economically marginal.

The full transition took a couple of decades. Weyerhaeuser shut down its company town in 1956. Even gyppo mining stopped at Roslyn, Cle Elum, and Newcastle in 1963. A second bridge was built across Lake Washington. Boeing kept growing. Many rail lines were abandoned; on others, trains became few and far between. The I-5 freeway was completed through Seattle in 1965. The 1962 Seattle World's Fair, with the theme "Century 21," came at a genuine time of transition.

The late 1960s were another economic boom time for the Puget Sound region. More than one hundred thousand people worked at Boeing. Even though Boeing laid off two-thirds of its workforce between 1969 and 1971, pushing statewide unemployment to 15 percent, the economy never turned back to the traditional resource industries, and a majority of voters never turned back to the old frontier mentality of growth at any price.

By that time it was clear that some of the places people had taken for granted for generations wouldn't be around for Century 21 if nothing was done to save them. In Seattle the nineteenth-century brick buildings of Pioneer Square were saved as a historic district in 1970. The Pike Place Market, which would have been destroyed by a massive urban renewal project, was saved by initiative in 1971. New freeways that would have sliced through city neighborhoods were blocked by voters. People who lived near the old, seldom-used Seattle, Lake Shore and Eastern right-of-way started working to get it transformed into a trail. At the rail line's western end, the old gasworks on the shore of Lake Union was being made into a city park. Voters passed the Forward Thrust bond issues. Hikers and environmentalists persuaded the federal government to create the North Cascades National Park in 1968 and worked to preserve the Alpine Lakes area in the mountains between Snoqualmie and Stevens passes. The Alpine Lakes Wilderness was created in 1976. In that same year the state legislature created the Mount Si Conservation Area, and, at around the same time, Harvey Manning and a small group started working to save natural areas in the Issaquah Alps of Cougar, Squak, and Tiger mountains from development.

The mid- and late 1980s were another boom period in the Seattle area. Boeing's workforce climbed back over one hundred thousand, high-

The Northwest has a history of saving places that help define its character. *Left:* In the 1960s, planners wanted to turn the Pike Place Market into a faceless urban renewal project. *Bottom:* Seattle citizens saved the market by passing an initiative in 1971, and today it looks much as it did when this picture was taken in 1959.

tech industries set up shop near Redmond and Woodinville, and Bellevue acquired a high-rise skyline.

The boom did not extend to the old mills or to the communities that depended on them. The sawmills at Preston and Snoqualmie didn't survive the decade. But the urban economy wasn't affected by the shutting down of sawmills, and as more people moved into the Seattle metropolitan area, development pressures grew exponentially. In 1989, just a year before the first Mountains to Sound March, the new bridge and tunnel linking I-90 to downtown Seattle were opened, greatly increasing the freeway's capacity to move people between the city and the still-rural land to the east. Commuters drove to the Seattle area from as far east as Cle Elum. Developers advertised locations along I-90 by saying that the freeway now represented the largest underused transportation corridor in the region. People who wanted to save habitat and trails and views and access points in the greenway corridor realized that the newly completed freeway was like a force of nature, inexorably channeling growth toward and across Snoqualmie Pass. The tide of development was flowing eastward. They had no illusions about stopping it. That wasn't the point. But if they were going to save and connect critical places along the greenway, they had a sense that it was now or never.

Opposite: Creating an understanding and appreciation of our region's history is an important goal of the greenway campaign. Working with institutions like Seattle's Museum of History and Industry and local historical societies, the Mountains to Sound Greenway Trust plans a series of interpretive centers along the greenway route. These artist renderings show two proposals: a slow-speed route along the Sunset Highway, and a forestry museum that will inform and educate visitors about the history and present-day uses of logging in the region.

Chapter V

Wilderness Close to the City

It's all so close. Less than an hour from Seattle you turn off the freeway at Denny Creek, drive a few, slow miles through the woods, and pass a section of the old wagon road over the mountains. The old road looks narrow—there are no carpool lanes, no passing lanes, just a minimal track through the trees. You can see why Daniel Gilman dismissed it in 1884 as "little more than a trail." Most of the trees beside the road are second growth, but at least one monster must have shaded the creaky wagons and the famished herds of Kittitas County cattle hurrying downhill toward the fat lands of the Snoqualmie Valley.

Beyond the wagon road, past Denny Creek, where green, foaming water has molded the rocks of the streambed into smooth curves, you find the trail to the Melakwa Lakes. Soon you pass massive cedars that probably stood there when Arthur Denny himself plodded into the woods, following his dream of iron ore and riches. You come back to modern reality in a hurry: in the shade of the big trees, you pass the huge concrete pylons that support the elevated westbound lanes of I-90 and hear traffic overhead. The effect is surreal: a freeway in the forest. (Elevating roads in strategic spots instead of blasting and gouging routes through mountainsides—as was done for the eastbound lanes on the opposite side of this valley—is a greenway goal.) Traffic noise has barely faded when a wooden sign announces that you're entering the Alpine Lakes Wilderness.

Instead of the freeway you soon hear the rush of water and look down through the trees at Denny Creek tumbling over rocks. The trail crosses the creek on a log bridge. Just upstream the water flows over a broad slab of granite. You can climb down to the gray slab, sit in the sun, eat lunch, let kids put their feet in the water. You're neither in the stream nor on the bank; you and the water share the same space.

The trail climbs. You hear falling water again as the stream foams over a short drop, slides smoothly over slick granite, and plunges airily to the

Only an hour's drive from Seattle, trails like this one near Denny Creek lead hikers into the Alpine Lakes Wilderness. Hikers and environmentalists from both sides of the Cascades worked for years to protect national forestland north of I-90 as wilderness. In 1976 Congress set aside 363,000 acres.

Freeways can be built through mountains and forests without blasting and bulldozing the slopes and trees. The westbound lanes of I-90 near Denny Creek are a good example of what can be done. Elevating the roadway is more costly but has much less impact on the landscape, and hikers and wildlife can pass freely beneath the road.

rocks below. At the lakes themselves, the water is icy and clear. A big tree on a far bank has snapped like kindling in a winter storm. (Winter is hard on trees in the western Cascades, which is one reason why timberline is found at such low elevations there. On the Cascades' eastern slopes, where winters bring less snow and summers are warmer, the treeless alpine zone begins fifteen hundred feet higher.) Early in the season, snow still clings to the surrounding mountains and rings the upper lake. Across the lower lake, Chair Peak rises abruptly from the shore. This is the peak on which Denny found iron, the same iron Daniel Gilman dreamed of hauling when he built the Seattle, Lake Shore and Eastern Railroad, and Peter Kirk dreamed of refining when he started to build a steel mill at Kirkland. You'd never know it now. The industrial dreams of the nineteenth century are long gone. It would be hard to find a more peaceful spot.

People have been hiking in the Alpine Lakes area for generations, and by now so many hike there that some trails and campsites are overused. The area has been formally protected only since 1976. It took eight years of work by citizen activists on both sides of the Cascades to get the federal legislation introduced and passed. Congress had created the North Cascades National Park in 1968, and another national park in western Washington clearly wasn't in the cards. Instead, the federal government protected 363,000 acres north of I-90 as the Alpine Lakes Wilderness.

Climbing out of the Denny Creek area on the steep trail up Granite Mountain, it's hard to imagine that anyone would seriously consider *not* protecting this landscape. You gain altitude quickly, and if you look back to the south you soon see the white cone of Mount Rainier appear over the

Encountering the huge concrete pylons of an elevated highway in the forest is a surreal experience, but large cedar trees grow undisturbed around them, and a short hike up the trail there's no trace of the freeway. The Mountains to Sound Greenway Trust hopes to encourage more of this kind of construction, especially as rural routes are widened to accommodate more highway travel.

The Granite Mountain trail offers spectacular views and is known for an abundance of wildflowers early in the season and for delicious huckleberries in the fall. But this and other scenic hikes in the Alpine Lakes are now so popular that overcrowding is often a problem. By providing more recreation and hiking opportunities along the greenway corridor, connecting existing trails and increasing their accessibility to urban dwellers, some high-country use can be dispersed, reducing overuse and preserving wildness.

nearest ridge. As you climb, Rainier grows and grows until finally you can see the entire mountain, from base to summit.

Across the way are Rattlesnake Mountain and other nearby peaks. You can also see mile after mile of clearcut slopes. The higher you climb, the more logged ridges you see. Everyone is impressed by the view of Rainier. A lot of people are also appalled by the obvious extent of the logging.

Logging is, of course, nothing new in these mountains. But the historical pattern here and elsewhere has been for loggers to start at lower elevations, where the trees are more accessible, and work their way up the slopes. By now loggers are working the upper slopes, where the cutting is visible for miles. In some areas the pace of logging accelerated during the 1980s, increasing the number of visible clearcuts.

Early in the season, wildflowers crowd the trail; higher up, marmots scamper across the lingering snow. Around Labor Day you walk through acres of huckleberries with red leaves and blue fruit; it's hard to make much progress on the trail when you stop every few steps for another taste.

The landscape isn't totally benign; the slopes are steep, the rocks massive, and if you climb too early in the year, you run a serious risk of dying in an avalanche. Still, Granite Mountain is accessible, and a lot of people climb it. If you talk with some of them, you're likely to find people who really love these mountains: a young man who grew up hiking here, went east to graduate school, and now crams all the hiking he can into summer visits; an older man whose job at Boeing didn't give him much time to get out on the trails, so he took early retirement and now spends a lot of his days wandering through the mountains.

They all come for the view. On a clear day you can see in all directions. To the south, you see not only the full, perfect cone of Rainier, but also the tip of 12,000-foot Mount Adams. To the east, you see Mount Stuart and the Stuart Range, the western sides of the peaks that rise behind Cle Elum. North, you see 10,500-foot Glacier Peak and the North Cascades.

The northern peaks look different from those to the south: they show more exposed rock, more granite spires, battlements, crenellations. This isn't just an illusion. Arthur Kruckeberg writes in *The Natural History of Puget Sound Country* that "the North Cascades (north of Snoqualmie Pass) are a jumble of highly deformed, intensively metamorphosed sedimentary, plutonic and metamorphic rocks. . . . Rocks like granites, diorites, schists and gneisses seen here are as spectacular as any in the world. The Washington Cascades to the south of the pass, on the other hand, are a 'slag pile' of volcanics thousands of meters thick, which effectively mask the older rocks and structures from our view."

The Cascades run from south of Lassen Peak in California to the Fraser River in British Columbia. The character of the whole seven-hundred-mile range changes at Snoqualmie Pass. There's no obvious reason why this should be true—no fault line runs across the pass—but it is. The Cascades were pushed up when two tectonic plates crunched together. The rocks north of the pass were pushed higher than those to the south. Presumably all the mountains were covered by volcanic rock at one time, however the North Cascades have been scoured by wind and rain and stressed by freezing and thawing at higher elevations. Exposed to harsher conditions for millions of

years, the new volcanic rock has eroded off the northern peaks, while south of the pass it has survived.

Looking east from the crest of Granite Mountain, you can see the freeway snaking through the pass. The road heads uphill from the Puget Sound basin, climbing north toward Snoqualmie summit, then makes a big fishhook bend, and reaches the summit heading due south. This is counter-intuitive. The highway through the pass runs ultimately from the East Coast to the West Coast. The pass itself is the route from the east side of the Cascades to the west side. When you reach the summit and head down, you assume you're going east to west, but you're not. The road follows the contours of the land, and those contours force a traveler to sneak up on the compass points from odd angles and take the long way around.

Although the Cascades run north and south, the pass isn't the only geographical feature that doesn't run neatly east-to-west. The east-west collision of tectonic plates that produced the mountains was evidently skewed by another plate pushing from the south. The resulting stress created valleys that run northwest-southeast. Following these valleys, the Snoqualmie and other rivers flow generally northwest from the Cascade crest, and the Yakima flows southeast. These river courses were formed by the contours of the rock itself, not by the action of glaciers. The rivers probably followed their present courses long before the last glaciers arrived.

You can reflect plenty on the age of things if you walk the Pacific Crest Trail from Snoqualmie Pass, but you may start by thinking less about time than about distance. At the edge of the parking lot, as you start north from the pass, a wooden sign announces "Stevens Pass 67." It's a little like those highway signs in the remote inland West that say things like "Next gas 112 miles." You can walk all the way to Stevens Pass without crossing a road. If you don't mind a few road crossings, you can walk all the way to Canada. Or to Mexico. The Pacific Crest Trail runs from border to border. Heading east from Snoqualmie Pass, you can follow the John Wayne Pioneer Trail to Idaho. Ultimately, the trail may hook up with other trails that traverse the whole country. Snoqualmie Pass can be a crossroads of long-distance hiking.

The Pacific Crest Trail used to start at the edge of old Highway 10. A bus would drop you at the log-walled Summit Inn, and—after a stop for breakfast or coffee—you could walk a little way along the shoulder and start hiking. The right-of-way for the new freeway destroyed part of the hiking trail in the late 1960s. The old Summit Inn burned down around the same time. Hikers no longer start on the shoulder of the main road, but they don't have to go far from it to find the trailhead.

The trail itself plunges quickly into big trees. Even before you enter the Alpine Lakes Wilderness, two-foot-thick trunks are everywhere, three-footers are common, and some trunks are five or six feet across. Many of the trees are shaggy with moss. Underbrush grows among the trunks, but thinly, so the slopes above and below the trail are parklike. At one point a wide swath of trees has been mowed down by an avalanche—just a little reminder, should one be needed, that nature is bigger than you are.

Climbing quickly into the wilderness, you get glimpses through the trees of nearby peaks. Early in the year, snow still clings to sheltered spots, but on an open scree-slope the trail is lined with flowers: pink-purple heather,

A rare view of the Cascades without snow cover in the dry summer of 1992. The mountains north of Snoqualmie Pass were tilted higher by geological forces than the mountains farther south and have been shaped by wind and weather to form a landscape of sharp granite cliffs and crags.

The Pacific Crest Trail crosses under the freeway at Snoqualmie Pass. Hikers or horseback riders can follow the trail all the way from Canada to Mexico. The John Wayne Pioneer Trail, which runs across Washington and may some-day connect to trails across the entire United States, also crosses the Cascades at Snoqualmie Pass, making it a crossroads of long distance hiking.

pale phlox, white beargrass, orange-red paintbrush, red columbines with yellow centers, and many others, all in the same short stretch.

On a slope above the trail, where clumps of heather bloom among the boulders and yellow lichen dapples the rock, you can see mountains all around. If the day is cloudy, fog fills the gaps between the ridges, as if the image had been compressed by a telephoto lens. The base of a mountain disappears into the clouds, rising almost infinitely in your imagination. The peaks drift in and out of view. This is when the Cascades look most like Chinese landscape painting: the vertical crags, the drifting mist, the dark conifers dotting the slopes. There are no traveling monks, but the stippled surface of the mountainside across the way, all pale rock and dark vegetation, could have been made with brush strokes, with gouts of ink that shape the underlying white space of the paper.

Looking over this scene, you know why John McPhee wrote in *Encounters with the Arch-Druid* that "a great many people believed [the Cascades] were the most beautiful mountains in the United States. A smaller and, on the whole, more parochial group felt . . . [they] were the most beautiful mountains in the world" (Farrar, Straus, and Giroux, 1971).

Hikers enjoy a wintry day on Tiger
Mountain, one of the Issaquah Alps.

Chapter VI

Saving the Issaquah Alps

The trail drops steeply past thick Douglas firs and levels out in marshland near a clear, shallow stream. Huge boulders, monoliths fallen from the cliffs above, are covered by hanging gardens of moss and ferns. Close to the stream, blackened by some long-dead fire, a fragment of a cedar snag, shard of the old forest, rises ten feet above the marsh. The stream is all you hear. There are no people, no fences, no roads, no cars.

Urban civilization could be a hundred miles away, or a thousand. But it's not. This is the east side of Cougar Mountain, which stretches west into the residential neighborhoods of Bellevue. There may still be occasional bears and even cougars on Cougar Mountain, but there are also a lot of expensive tract homes. The tide of development has long since engulfed the mountain's western flank and has made serious inroads along its northern slopes. But the heart of the mountain has been preserved as a regional wildland park, and within an easy walk of the freeway one can still find solitude. That wouldn't have been true without Harvey Manning.

When Manning and his wife moved to the western slope of Cougar in 1952, it was virtually all undeveloped. It was certainly not virgin wilderness; coal had been mined there, people had lived on its lower slopes for nearly a century, and loggers had cut most of the old trees decades before. But coal mining had almost petered out by then, new trees had grown, a few of the old ones had escaped the loggers, and Cougar was still largely rural, beyond the city's gravitational pull. The Mannings assumed it would always stay that way. They were wrong.

Manning liked Cougar as a place to live, but as a serious mountain climber and hiker he disdained its easy slopes. In the early 1970s, though, as part of a struggle to give up smoking, he started taking long daily walks close to home. He began to appreciate Cougar and the nearby peaks of Squak and Tiger. They may not have been real high country, but you didn't have to drive for hours to reach them. Besides, they were wild enough so that walk-

ing through them a person could feel solitude, see wildlife, even get temporarily lost.

At about the time Manning started to appreciate the relative wildness of Cougar and its neighbors, he realized that it wouldn't last forever. It wouldn't even last much longer. The east side of Lake Washington was becoming a major population center, and houses were already climbing Cougar's western slopes.

How could even a portion of these close-in mountains be saved? The first step was to make people care about them. In 1976 Manning wrote an article for *Seattle Weekly* describing the virtues of Cougar, Squak, and Tiger mountains, christening them the "Issaquah Alps" and suggesting that they were worth saving. "Alongside Rainier, Shuksan or Olympus," he conceded, "these Alps wouldn't deserve rating as respectable foothills. Ah, but they are not alongside Rainier, Shuksan or Olympus. Forming the tip of a long finger of the Cascades poking far west from the axis of the range, they thrust deep into Metropolitan Seattle. . . . It's second growth wilderness. But many a time, leaving trails to explore green-gloomy depths of ravines, crawling over and under mossy logs, raked by salmonberry brambles and devil's club thorns, blundering shin-deep into the black ooze of skunk cabbage gardens, I've felt as intimately entangled with rude nature, as remote from peatmoss-and-patio-tamed suburbia as if I were battling up Luna Creek in the Northern Pickets. . . . When the world is too much with me and my powers lie wasted, I cannot escape in minutes, for pennies, to Shuksan and Big Beaver, to Rainier meadows or Hoh rainforest or Shi Shi Beach surf, or even our splendid backyard wilderness of the Alpine Lakes country. But I can make it to the Issaquah Alps. They are precisely where wilderness is needed most— close to the city's traumatized masses."

Opposite: Although development crowds the freeway at Issaquah, large areas of Cougar Mountain and neighboring Squak Mountain are still covered by comparatively unbroken second-growth forest. *Above:* The establishment of a wildland park on Cougar Mountain was controversial, and preserving its wildland character in the face of competing demands is a never-ending struggle.

The name Issaquah Alps had been used tongue-in-cheek, but it caught on and is now used without a trace of irony. It has given Cougar, Squak, and Tiger a stature they might not otherwise have had.

The idea of saving the Alps caught on, too. After the *Weekly* article and another that Manning published in the *Seattle Times* appeared, a few people with similar ideas called him. They all wanted to save what was left of the relatively wild country in the Alps. In 1979 a small group got together in Issaquah's Rollin Log tavern and decided to form the Issaquah Alps Trails Club. That meeting began the organized effort to save the Issaquah Alps.

Early members of the Trails Club knew that bringing people into the Alps to see for themselves what was at risk would be the most effective way of winning allies. In Manning's words, "Every time someone takes a walk, that is, in a sense, a vote." For political reasons they started to build hiking trails. They named places, led hikes, wrote guidebooks.

They also got involved in more conventional politics. In the late 1970s King County launched a community planning process for the New-castle area, which included Cougar Mountain. A couple of club members served on the citizens committee that prepared the plan, and others lobbied and went to meetings. The club proposed a regional wilderness park on top of Cougar Mountain. The committee adopted the proposal unanimously, and the park became the heart of the plan. It was, however, a relatively radi-cal and controversial step. Some developers didn't like it, and they found sympathetic ears on the county council. When the plan reached the council, members made a number of changes. One was to tack development potential onto some of the land that the committee had designated as a park and to build a road right through it. Allowing the land to be developed in the future would have undercut the whole rationale for making it a park.

Committed to holding the line on urban growth but knowing that the move would touch off a great deal of controversy, then–County Execu-tive Randy Revelle vetoed the revised plan. Revelle's veto angered a lot of people. Things got pretty tense in the county's executive offices. The ques-tion became what kind of compromise could satisfy both sides. Manning and King County Planning Director Harold Robertson repaired to the Rollin Log with contour maps of Cougar Mountain to see what might work. The executive and legislative branches of county government negotiated, and the planning department created a third version of the plan. By the time the new plan reached the county council, a compromise had already been struck. The plan sailed through; this time it wasn't vetoed. One of its key provisions was the park. The King County brochure describing the finished plan stated flatly that "a regional wildland park of about two thousand acres . . . is a top priority."

The Cougar Mountain park wasn't the first piece of the Issaquah Alps to be saved as a natural area. A state wilderness park already stood on Squak Mountain to the east. Before World War II, Seattle attorney Stimson Bullitt was "wandering around in the hills and I found Squak Mountain and I was kind of charmed by it." He decided it would be a nice place to buy some land and build a vacation cabin, so "I went around to guys' doorsteps and I bought some parcels for $5 to $10 an acre." Then the United States entered World War II, and Bullitt spent four years in the Navy. When he

returned, he bought more land. Soon he had a complete section. His land had been logged, but the forest had grown back. An abandoned logging road enabled him to get there in a four-wheel-drive truck. Bullitt built a cabin but wound up not using it. The place was destroyed by vandals.

Having assembled but never really used the land, Bullitt put it in trust for his children. When they got old enough to receive title to the property, they wondered what to do with it. Bullitt said they had several options: they could build on the property and live there themselves; they could sell it, most likely to a developer; or they could donate it as a park. None of Bullitt's children liked the idea of having the property developed, but none wanted to live there. They went along with the idea of a park. Bullitt then drafted a deed for the state parks department. The Squak Mountain property would be a wilderness park: there would be no structures, no roads, no motorized vehicles; if the state violated the conditions, it lost the land. The state accepted Bullitt's terms, and the Squak Mountain wilderness park was born. In places the park touches the backyards of suburban houses, and at the top it touches the road and towers of an antenna farm. But in the middle there are big trees and winding trails and silence. The stone chimney of Bullitt's old cabin still stands among the trees; the "Bullitt fireplace" has become a landmark.

East of Squak, on Tiger Mountain, the state owned a lot of land, but none of it was park. The land was managed by the state Department of Natural Resources (DNR), which had a constitutional obligation to make money off it for the state public school trust and no plans for Tiger Mountain except selling timber. Tiger, which rises over Issaquah, had been logged decades before and, in the normal course of events, would simply be logged again.

While the DNR's duty to raise money for the schools was clear, the

Stimson Bullitt purchased a section of forest on Squak Mountain in the 1940s. His children subsequently gave it to the state for a wilderness park. The stone fireplace of a house Bullitt built on the mountainside has become a landmark. *Top:* Hikers can enjoy the deep woods on Squak Mountain on trails built by members of the Issaquah Alps Trails Club.

A common sight from I-90 almost any day of the year is the cars lined up at High Point, near the Tradition Lake plateau on the north side of Tiger Mountain. Quick access from the nearby cities of Bellevue, Redmond, and Seattle and a wide variety of trails make Tiger Mountain a popular family hiking area. The Tradition Lake trailhead is the busiest in the state. The Mountains to Sound Greenway Trust wants to create more recreational opportunities close to where people live and make them accessible by Metro bus.

agency did not have to turn a blind eye to all other uses of Tiger Mountain. And the mountain was already being used for other things. It was a natural: it provided wildlife habitat right at the edge of Issaquah, and it offered a very large, very accessible place for people to hike. Some of its trails lie an easy walk from downtown Issaquah. You can literally start on the town's main drag, walk out past the Rollin Log tavern and a Chinese restaurant toward the freeway entrance, and in minutes be climbing a steep trail onto Tiger Mountain. You can also start behind the high school or pull off the freeway at High Point, where all those cars mark the trailhead on any sunny day. In little more time than it takes to park, you can be on the Tradition Lake trail.

Members of the Issaquah Alps Trails Club worked from the start to get people walking on Tiger Mountain. They weren't the first. A high school English teacher named Bill Longwell had beaten them to it. Longwell had been building trails on Tiger and Squak mountains for years. (Before Longwell or anyone else built trails, hikers had followed old logging roads and railroads through the woods.) He and a friend had started on Squak in 1972, and two years later, when The Mountaineers decided to create a trail on Tiger Mountain, Longwell wound up in charge of the project. Students from his high-school classes helped. By the end of 1977 more than half of the first eleven-mile segment was already finished.

Longwell started building trails without a political motive, just because he liked to walk in the mountains. But the mood in the late 1970s was adversarial, and he agrees that trails equal hikers, who can equal votes. "If you didn't have those trails on Tiger you wouldn't have those two hundred cars parked at High Point every weekend," Longwell says. "Those two hundred cars forced the hand of every [land] manager [on Tiger Mountain]."

By now that process seems obvious. In the mid-1970s, though, Tiger Mountain's evolution into a hiking center didn't seem inevitable. Preserving large portions of Tiger Mountain for hiking and wildlife required fundamental changes in policy by the Department of Natural Resources. If the DNR was driven only by a desire to raise as much money as possible for the state's school construction fund, putting people on the trails wouldn't prevent massive clearcuts.

The DNR's leadership changed in 1980, though, with the election of Brian Boyle as Commissioner of Public Lands. Boyle was aware of the antagonism that had developed between environmentalists and the DNR and was eager to see the department try new forms of forest management near urban areas.

At the beginning of 1981, right after Boyle took office, Harvey Manning invited him to come and take a look at Tiger Mountain. The weather was terrible. Boyle refers to it as "my famous slog." On "a wet, disgusting day" they hiked up and looked around Tiger, then got out of the weather in the Rollin Log tavern, where they talked about what could be done.

Boyle subsequently had a citizens committee draw up a forest management plan that recognized the importance of trails and habitat, preserved stream corridors, and protected the mountain from wholesale clearcutting. Boyle's assistant, Bob Rose, drafted and lobbied through legislation enabling the DNR to set land aside permanently for conservation. Tiger Mountain wasn't the only candidate for conservation status, but it was an important one. The trick was to set some land aside forever without reducing the DNR's long-term ability to raise money for the public schools. The solution was for the legislature to earmark money from a real estate excise tax to buy timber rights on the land. The DNR would then use the money to buy productive timberland elsewhere. (Some land was set aside that way. The legislature subsequently repealed the real estate excise tax but has used budget surpluses to buy more timber rights and preserve more land.) At the waterfront rally that ended the 1990 Mountains to Sound March, Boyle announced that the state would set aside 840 acres on the northwest side of Tiger as a conservation area.

The same program has been used to expand the conservation area at Mount Si. The DNR acquired more of Si through exchanges with Weyerhaeuser and Georgia-Pacific, and then used state money to transfer the land from the school trust to conservation status. The agency also acquired land on Mount Washington and Mount Tenerife through exchanges with Weyerhaeuser, and the U.S. Forest Service has expanded the Alpine Lakes Wilderness in the same way. Weyerhaeuser, for its part, has been pursuing land exchanges for years. The company is frankly glad to trade land it owns in places where logging will be controversial for land that is likely to receive less public scrutiny and may also be better suited to growing trees.

By creating the conservation areas the DNR has protected some critical places and made it clear that earning money for the schools isn't the state's sole responsibility. But conservation areas are expensive—the Mount Si additions cost almost $15 million—and they add up to relatively little land. The big challenge remains managing the state's commercial forest in ways that are compatible with wildlife and hikers.

Conserving parts of the Issaquah Alps isn't quite like saving miles of

The management plan for Tiger Mountain State Forest reflects environmental, recreational, and economic values. Here former Commissioner of Public Lands Brian Boyle, a leader in the creation of the Mountains to Sound Greenway Trust, discusses the plan. The Tiger Mountain plan is a model of managed and productive forestry that combines revenue production with recreation and conservation.

ancient forest on the Olympic Peninsula or saving real wilderness in the North Cascades. Many of the main trails follow old logging roads or railroad grades, which makes it hard to pretend one is placing the first human footsteps in an undiscovered valley or exploring with Lewis and Clark.

But it doesn't diminish the experience. In the Spanish Pyrenees, even in national parks, one may wind up walking between lines of piled stones that mark the edges of old roads along which people have walked and driven livestock for centuries. The rock walls make it impossible to think of even high and remote country as real wilderness, but they create a sense of history, of the layers of history, that adds something valuable to the experience.

Besides, the accessibility of the Issaquah Alps is part of their value. You can walk to them or ride the bus. You can take along young children. People do. At the paved start of the Tradition Lake trail you may encounter a couple with a baby in a stroller. In the parking lot for the Wilderness Creek trail you may encounter two young women carrying babies in backpacks having their picture taken by an elderly couple they met in the lot; this is the babies' first hike, and the women want a photograph.

But if you're not toting a baby and you don't want to follow an old logging road, you can find steeper, narrower paths. You can walk alone for hours while the sound of running water blocks out all other noises or the wind sweeps through the treetops with a sound like surf. You can find remnants of the ancient forest, get your feet wet, lose the trail.

There are also spectacular views. Perhaps no views are more impressive than those from Rattlesnake Mountain, just east of Tiger, which forms a crucial link in the chain of forested mountains between Lake Washington and Snoqualmie Pass. The cliffs at the eastern end of Rattlesnake look over what used to be Rattlesnake Prairie, now part of the Cedar River watershed, to the western wall of the Cascades. The climb to that view can be a little tricky; the trail is steep and slippery in spots, requires some stepping on bare rock, and brings the hiker uncomfortably close to some sheer drops.

At the other end of Rattlesnake, all you have to do is get out of your car—or park it in the right direction—for the view. There, a very short drive from the freeway, the Snoqualmie Winery—now a wine-tasting room—occupies a site with a panoramic view of the valley east to the Cascades and north across the green fields of old Meadowbrook and Tollgate farms to Mount Si. You can't drive to a better view of this landscape. The site is owned by the city of Snoqualmie, which has brought in water and sewers and zoned it for industry. The city would like to preserve the view and the public's access, but it used federal money to lay the water and sewer lines, and if the winery site doesn't generate jobs, the money has to be repaid.

Most of Rattlesnake Mountain has been privately owned for generations, primarily by the Weyerhaeuser Company, and much of it is crisscrossed by logging roads. Virtually all of the ancient forest was cut long ago, and large parcels of second-growth timber have recently been clearcut. But Rattlesnake remains largely undeveloped. Protected on the south and west by the Cedar River watershed, it has tremendous value for wildlife, for hiking, and for the aesthetics of the I-90 corridor.

The Mountains to Sound Greenway Trust decided early that it would be critical to preserve Rattlesnake Ridge. Volunteers from the Issaquah Alps Trails Club started building trails on the steep northern slope, from the end of the main logging and powerline access road up to the ridge. And the Bullitt Foundation gave the Trust for Public Land money to take an option on Weyerhaeuser's ridgetop property, which enabled the trust to halt logging there until public funds could be found to buy the land.

In April 1992 Greenway Trust chairman Jim Ellis was invited to explain the greenway concept to the King County Council. Asked for the most helpful thing King County could do, Ellis suggested buying Rattlesnake Ridge. He was told the county didn't have money to buy the land right away. He knew that; he just wanted to get the idea into circulation. But the next week the council decided that putting up half the money needed to acquire Rattlesnake was a high priority—the state Department of Natural Resources was ready to put up some of the money and was trying to get enough additional

state funding to pay for half—and directed the King County executive to start working on it. Today the ridgetop still isn't publicly owned, but the wheels are turning.

From the ridge one can look south across the Cedar River watershed, over green hills that seem to go on and on forever. When Ellis and his brother climbed Rattlesnake Mountain more than fifty years ago—because even then everyone climbed Mount Si and they wanted to do something different—he was struck by that long, rolling, southward view. It hasn't changed much in the past half century.

The northward view has changed more, but—as from Mount Si— you can still make out distinct towns, open fields, the lines of rivers winding through. On a clear day you see north to Mount Baker and the peaks of the North Cascades, east to the mountains of Snoqualmie Pass, far west to the Olympics. Across the valley is Mount Si, with the low, flat-topped berm of Grouse Ridge clinging to its rocky side. It is one thing to know in the abstract that Grouse Ridge is a moraine left by the last glacier, but quite another to *see* Grouse Ridge as a pile of rock and soil pushed up the valley by moving ice. From the north side of Rattlesnake you can see it as a moraine, and the dry fact becomes real: this ridge blocking the head of the valley used to mark the leading edge of a river of ice.

With a little imagination you can picture the tops of Si and Rattlesnake rising above the blue glacial ice, much as the summit of Mount Rainier sometimes floats above a layer of clouds. With a little imagination you can also look forward and see them rising from a sea of urban sprawl. It is critical to save the peaks. But it is not enough.

Opposite: Rattlesnake Mountain is a crucial link in the chain of mountains between Lake Washington and Snoqualmie Pass. A steep trail leads up the mountain from the southeast and provides spectacular views toward Seattle's Cedar River watershed. The Mountains to Sound Greenway Trust plans a cooperative venture with the city of Seattle to improve trails to Rattlesnake Ledge and create new trails along the watershed's boundary, west to Tiger Mountain and east toward Snoqualmie Pass. *Above:* Rattlesnake Mountain has been logged for generations, but to halt further logging and expand recreational opportunities, the Bullitt Foundation gave the Trust for Public Land money to purchase an option on the mountain's ridgetop land. The addition of this land to the greenway corridor will help provide linked trails along the entire length of the greenway.

Chapter VII

Citizens and Public Money Built a Trail

By 1971 the tracks that curved north around Lake Washington on Daniel Gilman's old Seattle, Lake Shore and Eastern right-of-way—then owned by the Burlington Northern—were seldom used. Through trains had avoided them since 1963. Plants grew thickly beside the rails, and in summer blue vetch bloomed. All year round, twice a week, an old steam locomotive pulled a single carload of coal to a University of Washington power plant. The old engine was so slow and noisy and blew its whistle so frequently that even parents of young children who lived near the tracks around Northeast 93rd Street in north Seattle didn't consider it much of a threat. They did worry about the high, unfenced crossing over Sand Point Way, so if young children used the tracks as a pathway to Matthews Beach at the northern end of Lake Washington, a parent always went along. Virtually everyone in the neighborhood used the tracks to reach Matthews Beach: teenagers who swam and hung out at the beach all summer; their younger siblings; their parents. In winter people walked there to watch the Christmas ships. It was awkward to walk on the ties, but if you weren't shepherding a little kid, the trip took only five minutes or so. With small children, it might take fifteen.

The 93rd Street neighborhood formed a close community in the early 1970s. People socialized together and all knew each other's kids. When Seattle's KING-TV aired a pioneering series of documentaries on the Puget Sound region's environmental future and encouraged people to watch and discuss it in groups, it was natural for people who lived in the Northeast 93rd Street area to form a group of their own. When they talked about what they could do to improve things in their neighborhood, making the old railroad right-of-way into a bicycle and walking path seemed natural, too.

Everyone in the neighborhood lived within a couple of blocks of the tracks. They all had heard that Burlington Northern was thinking about abandoning the tracks and worried that the right-of-way would simply be sold to the adjacent property owners. As one member of the group, Mamie

A frosty morning jog along the Sammamish Trail.

Top: In the 1970s, community activists campaigned to have the old Seattle, Lake Shore and Eastern Railroad right-of-way along Lake Washington made into a city trail. Here marchers set out from the old gasworks at the north end of Lake Union—now Gas Works Park—for a rally held to promote the creation of what is now the Burke-Gilman Trail.

Bottom: A lot of people who lived along the Burke-Gilman's proposed route fought against the creation of a trail. They feared that crime rates would rise and property values would fall. Time has proven them wrong.

Rockafellar, recalls, "The idea came up, since it was a corridor, why not make it into a public-use corridor? Especially since it went from one park to another, why not save it as a linear park?" The route was already used by walkers and seemed a natural for bicycles. The actual right-of-way was obviously wider than the rails. There should be room for everyone.

This was such a logical idea that other people had thought of it, too. A group of people at the University of Washington and some Seattle city planners had talked in the 1960s about using the route as a trail after the railroad gave it up. *Footloose Around Puget Sound*, published by The Mountaineers in 1969, described the old rail line and called it an "oughter be"— that is, a route that oughter be a trail.

Still, nothing had been done to make the idea a reality. The 93rd Street group decided to do it or—since it wasn't the kind of neighborhood project they could do themselves with rakes and shovels—to get it done.

"It seemed like all we had to do was announce it and things would happen," says Jim Todd, who became the first president of the Burke-Gilman Trail Committee. That wasn't the way things worked in real life. Converting the railroad tracks to a pathway for walkers and cyclists—what has since become known as a "rails to trails" conversion—wasn't a sure thing. As Rockafellar says, "It was a seven-year haul."

If the Burlington Northern Railroad stopped running trains along the tracks, it might want to sell the right-of-way, not turn it over to the public. The city of Seattle, the University of Washington, and King County, which had jurisdiction over the route, might not be interested either. People who lived along the tracks might not want a trail running past their yards.

Members of the neighborhood group started by doing research to find out exactly which jurisdictions and whose property rights were involved. When they found that the right-of-way had originally been donated to the railroad by private property owners, they figured it was reasonable to argue that the railroad should donate it back to the public. They began lobbying public officials and lining up allies. Cycling was becoming popular—the new trail would provide a route for both recreational cyclists and commuters— and the group quickly won support from the Cascade Bicycle Club. Other allies included the Sierra Club and the Floating Homes Association.

The question of what the railroad would do with the right-of-way was settled after the group got late Senator Warren Magnuson, then chair of the Senate Commerce Committee, to write a letter to the Interstate Commerce Commission about the project. A railroad company can't abandon a line without ICC approval. In a move that has had national significance, the ICC decided that whenever a rail line is abandoned, local government must have the right of first refusal, a chance to turn the old rail bed into a trail for bikes or walkers.

The university, eager to encourage bicycle commuting, supported the idea enthusiastically. The chief executives of Seattle and King County supported it, too. A critical demonstration of public support for the project was a rally, co-sponsored by the trail committee and the Cascade Bicycle Club, that was held at Matthews Beach. Marchers started from either end of the 12.1-mile proposed trail and met at the park, which lay roughly in the middle. Seattle Mayor Wes Uhlman marched to the rally from the south end

Open fields that border the Sammamish Trail were preserved by public purchase of land and development rights with money from the Forward Thrust and Farmlands Preservation bond issues passed in 1968 and 1979. Citizens of the region have repeatedly voted to tax themselves to preserve the features that make this a special place to live and work.

Opposite: Horseback riders, as well as runners, walkers, and cyclists, use the Sammamish Trail.

and King County Executive John Spellman marched there from the north; both spoke at the rally. The project was no longer just a neighborhood issue. In 1972 Seattle made the Burke-Gilman route a "priority corridor" in its Comprehensive Bikeway Plan.

But it still wasn't a sure thing. Property owners along the route wanted the right-of-way themselves. They certainly didn't want a bicycle and walking trail bringing thousands of strangers past their homes. They saw the trail as a getaway route for criminals. Some people actually counted the number of bedroom windows that faced the trail. With the fear of crime came a fear that property values would drop. Those nice neighborhoods would become places in which nice people wouldn't want to live. The opposition was strong and very emotional. The city and the county had to choose between respecting opponents' fears and forcing people who lived nearby to accept a trail they didn't want.

The trail won. City and county governments finally approved the 93rd Street neighborhood's idea. But they didn't have the money to pay for it. They had nothing more than an abandoned railroad track. When Stan Unger had followed the trail in 1975 on his hike from Puget Sound to Snoqualmie Pass, he had to detour around a slide north of Matthews Beach. In the mid-1970s a newspaper article observed that "from one point of view the city has acquired an 11-mile-long blackberry patch. . . . Brambles have yielded several seasons of fruit while city wheels have turned slowly with money and land use planning concerning the trail." Nothing happened until $150,000 of Forward Thrust bond money was channeled to the project. Forward Thrust ultimately contributed nearly half a million dollars to the trail. Other funds came from Community Development Block Grants and the

An estimated 1.2 million people a year follow the Burke-Gilman Trail, and overcrowding has become a problem. Heavy traffic and conflicts among different types of users may make it necessary to separate people on wheels from people on foot. Though expensive, building separate, parallel trails may be the best solution.

Federal Urban Aid System. The trail was the first bicycle and pedestrian route in the nation that got federal gasoline tax money. Nineteen seventy-eight marked the formal opening of what is by now widely known as the Burke-Gilman Trail.

The fears of crime and plunging property values proved false. A 1987 study by the Seattle Engineering Department found that crime had not increased more in areas near the trail than it had increased elsewhere and that property values had risen. A few burglars had indeed made their geta-ways along the trail, but "police officers interviewed stated that there is not a greater incidence of burglaries and vandalism of homes along the trail. They attribute that fact to the absence of motor vehicles." One of the officers ex-plained that "teenagers have an umbilical cord of about 30 feet between them and their cars. There will not be significant trail problems as long as parking lots are away from the trail and bollards prevent motor vehicle use."

People advertising houses in the area now actually use proximity to the trail as a selling point. Jim Todd, who remembers the bitter fights with neighborhood groups, says, "I just love seeing that when people sell their houses on the Burke-Gilman Trail, they advertise it. 'On the trail' seems to increase property values." The Seattle engineering study found that "prop-erty near but not immediately adjacent to the Burke-Gilman Trail is signifi-cantly easier to sell and, according to real estate agents, sells for an average of 6 percent more as a result of its proximity to the trail. Property immediately adjacent to the trail . . . is only slightly easier to sell."

In the meantime the trail has helped set a national precedent. It wasn't the first rails-to-trails conversion in the country, but it was the first big, visible one. There are now more than four hundred converted rail lines in the United States.

The original 12.1-mile segment has been extended eastward by addi-tion of the Sammamish Trail, which doesn't quite meet the Burke-Gilman yet, but which allows a cyclist or walker, after only a short plunge through city traffic, to follow the Sammamish River all the way to Redmond's Mary-moor Park at the edge of Lake Sammamish. A westward extension leads along the Lake Washington Ship Canal to the Ballard locks.

Farther east more abandoned rail lines have been made into trails. One is the Preston-Snoqualmie Trail, a paved pathway that leads from the old logging town of Preston, just off the freeway, to a view of Snoqualmie Falls. The Preston-Snoqualmie Trail is wide open and easily graded, not the kind of path through the forest that one follows on Cougar or Tiger moun-tains, much less in the Alpine Lakes Wilderness. Yet it too takes a walker or cyclist away from cars, past massive gray stumps of the old forest, among sizable maples and firs. At the eastern end of the trail you can see Snoqual-mie Falls plunging into its granite basin with Mount Si as a backdrop. The roar of falling water is audible from a mile and a half away. A little to the west you can sit on a bench and look across the Snoqualmie Valley to the varicolored blocks of trees—each age group a different height and a slightly different shade of green—in Weyerhaeuser's Snoqualmie tree farm, while a pileated woodpecker hammers on a nearby snag.

A more ambitious rails-to-trails conversion is the John Wayne Pioneer Trail, which follows the abandoned Milwaukee Railroad right-of-way from eastern Washington to Snoqualmie Pass, then west from the pass to North Bend. After the Milwaukee Railroad went bankrupt at the end of the 1970s, the state Department of Natural Resources acquired almost all of its Washington right-of-way. In 1984 a twenty-five-mile segment between Easton and Cle Elum became part of the state park system. In 1990 the legislature gave the parks department control of everything between Cle Elum and the Columbia River.

When AT&T bought the old Milwaukee line between North Bend and Easton as a right-of-way for fiber optic cables, it gave that land, too, to the state parks department. You still can't walk all the way from North Bend to Easton on the old rail line—trestles are missing and a two-mile tunnel through the Cascades is closed to the public—and you have to detour on city streets or county roads at places farther east. In eastern Washington you need permission from the Department of Natural Resources. But eventually, with few interruptions, it could be possible to walk, ride horseback, or cycle across the state along the route of the last transcontinental railroad.

The Burke-Gilman Trail already makes it possible to walk or cycle from the heart of the city to open country. "It looks like a trail," says the *Seattle Best Places* guidebook, "but in spirit it's a park that provides a lush corridor of green from Gas Works Park on Lake Union to Kenmore's Logboom Park at the northern tip of Lake Washington." The gasworks on Lake Union was built in 1904 to turn coal from Newcastle into gas to light Seattle streets and homes. The plant kept producing gas—along with smoke and odors—until 1956. In the early 1970s the city of Seattle used Forward Thrust bond money to turn the old industrial site into a park, which opened two years before the formal opening of the Burke-Gilman Trail.

Gas Works Park, with its unobstructed view over Lake Union to the Seattle skyline, its grassy artificial hills, its rusting iron tanks and towers studded with rivets and gauges echoing the industrial past, immediately became popular with picnickers, kite flyers, and thousands of other people. Its view of the skyline made it an appropriate starting or ending point for a trail from or to the city. Its assemblage of towering, rusted industrial structures made it appropriate, too, for the origin or destination of a trail built along the right-of-way of a railroad that was originally built to haul iron and coal.

From Gas Works Park the trail winds past warehouses and loading docks to the University of Washington campus, past the power plant to which trains still brought coal in the early 1970s, through the dense residential neighborhoods northeast of the university, past the backyards of lakefront homes. Sometimes you see the flowering trees and shrubs in people's yards, sometimes the overgrown banks of ferns and brush that you'd expect on a walk along any old railroad line.

At present the Burke-Gilman trail ends in Kenmore's Logboom Park, beyond which you get a quick dose of urban reality—cars, motorcycles, stoplights, cement mixers rumbling by on city streets—before you pick up the Sammamish Trail. From here the trail follows the shallow, channeled water of the Sammamish River through parks and parklike settings out into open country. Long before the trail reaches Marymoor Park, although the high ground to the north and south is covered with houses and high-tech office buildings, you pass tractors and green fields. Cyclists, joggers, and

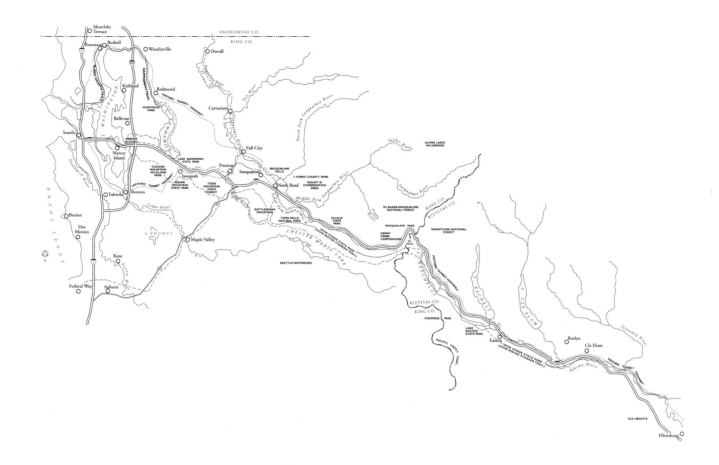

Expanding and connecting trail systems within the greenway corridor will become increasingly important as future growth and development occur and more people move to now-rural communities. The solid red lines indicate existing trails. The dotted red lines show some of the additions and connections that have been proposed by numerous individuals, organizations, and government agencies as part of the planning process for the Mountains to Sound Greenway.

walkers—traveling with kids, with dogs, with each other—are a lot closer than the cars on distant route 520.

It's startling to find so much open space in this area, and you wouldn't find it here if the public hadn't bought one thousand acres of Sammamish Valley farmland with money from the 1979 Farmlands initiative. Actually, the whole route is a catalog of public investment. Forward Thrust money developed Marymoor Park and bought the land on both sides of the Sammamish River. Metro laid a sewer line along the east side of the river and, in exchange for a cheaper easement, built the trail on top of it. Very few people remember all that. But a lot of people are familiar with the results.

The first inside photograph in *Greenways for America* (Johns Hopkins Univ. Press, 1990) shows a lone cyclist rolling through green fields on the Sammamish Trail. The only thing wrong with that picture is that a cyclist on the Sammamish or Burke-Gilman Trail is seldom alone. An estimated 1.2 million people use the Burke-Gilman Trail each year. It has helped make Seattle a place that, in 1990 and 1992, *Bicycling* magazine named the best cycling city in the United States and one of the five best cycling cities in the world. The city of Seattle's bicycle coordinator, Peter Lagerway, explains that "it's become a symbol of a large commitment to non-motorized facilities." By this time the problem is not lack of acceptance by the neighbors (although proposals to open new urban trails elsewhere still cause anxiety and draw protest), but over-use: people complain about traffic and worry about conflicts among fast cyclists, slow cyclists, roller skaters, runners, joggers, walkers, and people pushing strollers, all moving at different speeds. Clearly, on the Burke-Gilman and other popular trails it will be necessary to separate people on wheels from people on foot. In some cases it will probably be a good idea—albeit a costly one—to build separate, parallel trails. Ideally, recreational athletes will develop an ethic that prevents phalanxes of high-speed bikers from terrifying or actually injuring elderly walkers; until that happens, physical separation seems the best bet.

Despite the conflicts, people of all speeds use the Burke-Gilman Trail. The routes to and through the university and the weekend excursion to the Chateau Ste. Michelle winery have become standards. "It's a classic case," Jim Todd says. "There was so much opposition to it in the beginning and now it's universally regarded as a great success." Harvey Manning observes in *Footsore 1* (The Mountaineers, 1987), a guide to hikes in the Issaquah Alps and other places around Puget Sound, that "no list of America's great urban trails omits the Burke-Gilman." (The recent antagonism between bikers and walkers has given him second thoughts.)

Peter Lagerway says that "the spinoff has been incredible." Where trails are being developed around western Washington, "you'll find a citizens group behind each one, and Burke-Gilman is the inspiration for all of them." Its influence goes far beyond the borders of the state. Since the *Bicycling* articles came out, Lagerway gets calls just about daily from people all over the country who want to start bicycle programs in their own communities; he sends out copies of a twelve-minute video that features the Burke-Gilman Trail. The bright idea of 1971 has become an institution.

The Burke-Gilman Trail brings walkers and cyclists right into the city. Originally, it ended at Gas Works Park, pictured at left, but an extension now leads west to Puget Sound.

Chapter VIII

Commercial Forestry Keeps the Land Unpaved

You see them almost everywhere: beside trails in the Issaquah Alps, on approaches to the Alpine Lakes, hidden in brush beside the freeway. The huge silver stumps are the relics, the monuments, the tombstones of the old forest. Sometimes new trees grow from them. Sometimes they are visibly crumbling back into the earth. Always they bear notches for the springboards on which men stood with axes and saws to cut the living trees. Those springboard notches are like the tracks of some extinct reptile, evidence of a life-form that vanished long ago.

The notched stumps tell more than one story: if they evoke the vanished forest, they also evoke the vanished logging—the years, the decades, the generations of men balancing on springboards to fall some of the largest trees that people have ever seen. By now the almost complete disappearance of the ancient forest in the greenway corridor may seem tragic, but the cutting of those huge trees with hand tools was an act of enormous chutzpah and tenacity, a genuine epic of human labor. (With the right eye—or the right imagination—you can still see those trees every day. "The deep woods turn, turn and turn again," Gary Snyder has written. "The ancient forests of the West are still around us. All the houses of San Francisco, Eureka, Corvallis, Portland, Seattle, Longview, are built with those old bodies.")

For better or worse, logging *is* the history of western Washington. Coal mining paid the bills in Roslyn and Cle Elum, Issaquah, Renton, and Newcastle. Farms filled most of the Snoqualmie Valley. But towns such as Preston and Snoqualmie wouldn't have existed without their mills, and the cities on and near Puget Sound all started out shipping logs or lumber. Even Seattle, which was never just a mill town, exported logs to begin with; Henry Yesler's sawmill was Seattle's first real industry, and the city subsequently prospered by supplying mill towns around the sound.

Outside the agricultural valleys, the non-urban economy of western Washington has relied on forest products. If you want to talk about cultural

Huge silver stumps like this one on Squak Mountain are constant reminders of the Northwest's history, its old forests, and the epic labors of early loggers.

continuity in rural areas, you have to talk about the commercial growing, cutting, and milling of trees. The eastward spread of population and white-collar jobs along I-90 is a recent phenomenon. Even now the commercial forestry zone of eastern King County outside federal land includes roughly one thousand square miles. No one knows just how much is covered by standing timber and how much is covered by stumps, but there are clearly a lot of trees. Weyerhaeuser's Snoqualmie tree farm alone covers 228 square miles, or about one-fifteenth of King County.

In much of this area, a "working landscape" means a landscape in which trees are harvested and grown. At times in the not-so-distant past, that harvesting has been so visually intrusive that people who do not necessarily support environmental causes have been outraged. Public reaction to the very visible clearcuts in the Snoqualmie Pass area has created pressure to change the laws and regulations of Washington's forest practices. The strong negative response to the clearcuts suggests that people care about the landscape they see from their cars and that, in some way, they consider the view a kind of public property, a phenomenon in which the public has a legitimate interest.

On federal land around the pass, the forests themselves are public property, and the public can choose to preserve them for aesthetics, for environmental reasons, or for recreation. By and large, the public is choosing to do just that. Much of the federal land near Snoqualmie Pass has been preserved in the Alpine Lakes Wilderness, and current forest management plans do not call for logging on any of the rest.

On private forestland, which is most of the forestland at lower elevations, and on state trust land that is dedicated to earning money for school construction, the story is different. There the alternative to logging isn't

Logging has shaped the region's landscape for more than a century. *Opposite:* In the 1920s, Snoqualmie Valley loggers were still cutting mammoth old-growth trees with crosscut saws. *Above:* The expansion of highly visible clearcuts in the 1980s helped create public pressure to change established ways of managing forests. The Mountains to Sound Greenway Trust believes that the presence of commercial forestry in the greenway helps preserve open land and that imaginative forestry practices can help to resolve conflicts.

Early tree farms relied on nature to grow new forests on cutover land. Today large forest landowners plant, thin, and prune new trees to obtain maximum growth and rapid regeneration. *Opposite:* Purple fireweed is visible in a fresh clearcut right away. New seedlings are hard to see for years. Maintaining profitable tree farms close to metropolitan areas keeps the landscape forested and provides relief from urbanization.

unbroken forest; it is development—houses, offices, malls, parking lots.

This is not a question of saving ancient forests. Unfortunately—and representatives of forest-products companies agree it's unfortunate—within the greenway corridor there is virtually no ancient forest left to save. The only surviving remnants of any size are already protected. The choice is whether or not to keep harvesting and growing younger trees.

Obviously, a hillside covered with young trees looks different from a hillside covered with asphalt or concrete. But the difference goes beyond aesthetics: a young forest retains more water than a mini-mall or subdivision does, preventing erosion that can lead to landslides and the silting up of streams. And it provides better wildlife habitat. A young forest can't provide the range of habitat an ancient forest does, just as it can't create the cathedral effect of four-hundred-year-old trees. But it can furnish food and shelter for animals that don't frequent parking lots or fenced backyards (or in some cases, old-growth forests). The cougars that travel to the edge of Bellevue are traveling through second- and third-growth trees. A young forest also fixes carbon from the air, helping to counter—however slightly—the buildup of carbon dioxide that may contribute to global warming. The amount of carbon taken up by all the commercial forest in eastern King County doesn't balance out the CO_2 generated by cars, factories, wood stoves, and other man-made sources in the Seattle metropolitan area, but it makes a small contribution, and it has some symbolic value. It is ironic for the United States to tell Brazil and other countries to save their forests from development if we continue to obliterate ours. Ultimately, "Do as we say, not as we do" isn't very persuasive. Growing forests in the greenway corridor would be one way—albeit a small and local one—of putting our money where our mouths are.

To the pioneers the notion that these forests needed preserving would have seemed bizarre. The pioneers took the forests very much for granted. The sea of huge trees they found in the Northwest seemed inexhaustible. Of course, it wasn't. As early as 1884 an official of the Port Blakely mill wrote that "the timber contiguous to the Sound is nearly exhausted." He was talking about the best clear, straight-grained timber, but to see timber of any variety "exhausted" at that time was remarkable. The same could not have been said of the timber farther east. In the approaches to Snoqualmie Pass there was no way to haul old-growth logs to the mills, no way to haul finished lumber or shakes to market, so no one had even started logging. In 1886 Daniel Gilman wrote that the route between North Bend and Snoqualmie Pass was "all the way through heavily timbered government land which is not yet surveyed."

It didn't take long to turn a lot of that forest into an ocean of stumps, too. Clarence Bagley, writing about east King County in the 1920s, observed, "It is a safe prediction that within ten years all mills which do not have large areas of standing timber . . . will have gone out of business. Our boasted heritage of inexhaustible forests is nearly dissipated. Unless the Federal government or the state takes over the gigantic task of reforesting, the lumber industry of Washington will ere long become a matter of past history."

Bagley was right about the ancient forests that loggers were cutting at the time he wrote. They did disappear. But forests didn't. And if commercial logging is the only process that takes trees off the land, they won't.

By now both law and self-interest force almost anyone who cuts trees commercially to replant. But some landowners see their self-interest in using land for something other than forestry and simply violate the law. Others

Loggers now use chain saws instead of crosscuts and axes, but they are part of a historical tradition that dates back to the nineteenth century. Logging practices are changing to make cutting less visible and to protect public resources. The U.S. Forest Service, the state Department of Natural Resources, and the forest-products industry are all experimenting with new methods in the greenway corridor. The state forest on Tiger Mountain is being used as a laboratory for some of them. It is managed on a sustained-yield basis: that is, the amount of timber cut cannot exceed the amount of timber grown.

convert land to different uses legally. Even if land isn't being used for anything else, at high elevations in western Washington, where trees grow slowly, reforestation has sometimes been a pleasant fiction; critics refer to logging the high country as "cellulose mining." But certainly where major corporations or public agencies manage land within the greenway corridor, logging is followed by replanting.

The largest tract of private forestland in the greenway corridor is Weyerhaeuser's Snoqualmie tree farm. (This includes the land that Weyerhaeuser once logged with electric machinery.) At first all that land was simply forest. When an acre was logged, it became stumps, and stayed that way until nature reseeded the cutover land. When Weyerhaeuser launched the national "tree farm" movement in the 1940s, the Snoqualmie land was designated a farm. To begin with, the name "tree farm" was largely symbolic; it usually meant only that a company planned to let trees grow back instead of selling or developing the land. When a company did replant, it dropped seeds from airplanes or planted nursery stock grown from seeds that had been collected in a different environment, and relatively few of the young trees survived. By the 1960s, though, forest-products companies had figured out how to improve the odds, and by now the survival rate is over 95 percent.

State law calls for replanting within two years. A major forest-products company generally replants within one. Until recently the first step was to bulldoze the branches, bark, stumps, and other debris into big piles and burn them. Now most of the slash is left on the ground, where it will eventually leach its nutrients back into the soil.

This doesn't make a fresh clearcut any less a scene of devastation. If an ancient forest evokes Europe's cathedrals, a clearcut, no matter what the age of the fallen trees, evokes its World War I battlefields. Visually a fresh clearcut is instant Verdun.

People seeing it tend to be repelled and horrified. They do not see the tree-planting crews walking through the slash carrying canvas sacks filled with bare-root seedlings, forcing their narrow-bladed shovels through the slash, making a hole, inserting a seedling, stamping the earth down tightly around the roots, stepping over a log, struggling up a slope, planting another. Walking, digging, bending, stamping all day long, the crews plant a new tree every ten feet.

From a distance you can't see the young trees, but up close you find them growing through the slash, reaching toward sunlight, green against the dead branches and scarred earth. Life does go on. Virtually all these little trees —grown from seeds gathered in the same watershed, started in nurseries with better soil than the forest itself provides, planted only before the dry season begins—will survive. They will be thinned and pruned. If the soil is good, someone driving by will see a carpet of bright green within six years (on poor soil it may take twice as long). The green will darken, and the trees will start losing their bushy lower limbs within twenty years. They will be cut again in perhaps half a century.

But the casual observer probably doesn't know the prognosis, doesn't know that what you see won't be all you get. Even if the observer does know, it is unlikely that he or she will consider a fresh clearcut a thing of beauty or find in it any hint of the continuity of life. If some commercial

On land owned by major forest-products companies, tree planters usually enter logged areas within a year. They plant as many as 450 trees per acre, placing each seedling in the ground by hand.

Inside the Weyerhaeuser tree farm near Snoqualmie, forestland is a cool, deep green. Second- and third-growth forests provide more than aesthetic pleasures: they retain water and prevent erosion that may cause landslides and silt in waterways; they furnish food and shelter for animals; and they help counter the buildup of carbon dioxide that may contribute to global warming.

forestry is going to continue in eastern King County, logging must somehow be made acceptable to the public at large. This requires a number of things. For one, forest-products companies must change their logging practices to make cutting less offensive to the public: smaller clearcuts on longer rotations; cuts that make some allowance for the natural contours of the land.

The state forest on Tiger Mountain is being used as a laboratory for some of these techniques. Until the 1980s the state Department of Natural Resources (DNR) was interested primarily in selling timber on Tiger Mountain as profitably as possible, and environmental groups were interested in stopping the timber sales. Opponents went to court and the timber didn't get sold. The state was frustrated. Environmentalists were apprehensive. No one was happy.

When public lands commissioner Brian Boyle took his rainy hike on Tiger Mountain with Harvey Manning, he "just came face-to-face with the issue of forestry on the fringes of development." Boyle had the DNR trade land with Weyerhaeuser to create a solid block of state forest on Tiger, and he put together a nineteen-member citizens committee to draft a forest management plan. The idea was that a working forest on the urban fringe had to be managed differently from one out in the boonies. Tiger would set an example. A lot of diverse interests were represented on the citizens committee, and many members—including the chairman, Harold Robertson—were skeptical about the chances of agreeing on anything that mattered. The committee went at it, though, and members finally agreed on a plan that the DNR accepted almost entirely. The state forest on Tiger would be managed on a sustained-yield basis; that is, the cutting of timber couldn't exceed the growth of timber. The DNR had been managing its statewide holdings for

Keeping some commercial forestry in the greenway corridor is vital. The biggest threat to forestland is its conversion to other uses, like residential and commercial development. An estimated ten thousand to thirteen thousand acres of King County forestland are being converted each year. The choice we face in parts of the greenway is not between periodic logging and permanent forests, but between periodic logging and the permanent loss of forests.

sustained yield since 1962, but it had never before tried to manage a single forest that way.

Under the plan drawn up by the citizens committee, Tiger will provide timber, wildlife habitat, and places to hike. Shooting and off-road vehicles are prohibited. When logging is done, clearcuts will be smaller than usual. Some areas with high environmental value, heavy recreational use, and low economic potential won't be logged at all. The rest will be managed on the basis of its five watersheds. No more than 20 percent of any watershed can be cut in any decade.

The whole package was "a very radical departure for DNR," says Bob Rose, who was hired by Boyle to manage the planning project. Boyle himself considers it a "great experiment."

People in both the DNR and the forest-products industry consider the Tiger Mountain State Forest an important example: it may help make logging on the urban fringe politically acceptable. And its location is critical: Tiger marks the western limit of King County's forest-production zone. Rose says that the state forest there makes "a very strategic declaration of where a certain form of land management begins." It creates "a presumption that land to the east of there should remain in forestry."

What happens on Tiger and in other state forests is crucial because, in the long run, there is no way to guarantee that privately owned land will remain forest. Public agencies don't have to worry as much about economics. They may resist the pressure to convert forestland into something more profitable, to convert every last tree into dollars. In the final analysis, private companies exist to make money, and environmental or aesthetic values can't be allowed to impinge too much on the bottom line. The fact is that an acre of second- or third-growth trees simply isn't worth as much money as an acre of houses or 43,560 square feet of retail space. The biggest long-term threat to these second- and third-growth forests is conversion of the land to other uses. If a private landowner has an opportunity to convert forestland to a more profitable use, odds are that the land won't continue to grow trees. The public can buy development rights to the land; if it doesn't, the difference between the land's value as forest and its value for other uses will exert constant pressure to change. Let housing developments march right up to the edge of private commercial forestland and, in time, the loss of forests will be inevitable. Boyle argues that it's important to keep forestland in large blocks so that the state or private owners will face less economic and political pressure to develop. The pressures—or inducements—are strong: at least ten thousand to thirteen thousand acres of King County forestland are being converted each year.

Even if forestland owners don't want to convert their land to other uses, suburban housing and commercial forestry don't make good neighbors. People do not want to see their neighborhood forest leveled even if it will grow back in forty years. They do not want to hear chain saws and bulldozers in the early morning. Slash burning—already greatly restricted by state air pollution laws—is basically impossible if people are living right next door. Commercial forestry on the urban fringe won't be politically acceptable unless development stays away from the trees.

And it probably won't be acceptable unless people are given a realistic choice. Along much of the urban fringe they must realize that they can't choose between periodic logging and permanent forest; they must choose between periodic logging and the permanent loss of forest. That choice may not be ideal, but it is the one we face.

Chapter IX

The Challenge to Save Our Future

A great deal has already been done. Land has been preserved in the Alpine Lakes Wilderness, on Mount Si, and on Cougar, Squak, Tiger, and Rattlesnake mountains; the Burke-Gilman, Sammamish, John Wayne, Preston-Snoqualmie, and other trails have been created; a new management plan for forestry on the urban fringe is being followed on Tiger Mountain; the U.S. Forest Service is managing thousands of acres for wildlife and recreation. What remains undone?

Plenty. The future of some large and significant areas remains very much in doubt. And the goal, after all, is not to save only isolated natural areas, historic sites, and trails; it is to create a network. It is not to save occasional views along the greenway corridor; it is to preserve the overall look and feel of the place.

In some cases this may involve saving land for the sake of the view. In others it may involve saving land primarily for hiking and other recreational uses. In still others, land may be saved only because it's valuable as wildlife habitat, whether or not people use it.

The unfinished business is crucial. We do not want trails without trailheads, patches of wildlife habitat that lead nowhere, historic sites that no one visits, structures along the freeway that make the valleys look like the worst of Los Angeles or New Jersey, or development that simultaneously obliterates open space and the identities of small towns.

There will have to be compromises. We'll have to give up fifty acres to save four hundred, accept a development we'd rather not see in order to avoid one that would be a real disaster. The goal is to create a vast, complex mosaic. The whole mosaic must hang together, but it doesn't absolutely need—and isn't likely to get—every last piece. Some land will be too expensive. Some development plans will be too far along. The mosaic's final shape may not be exactly what we envision.

And there may not be a final shape at all. Human communities and

Parts of the landscape along I-90 are safe from development. The challenge is to keep them from being isolated, to create continuous green pathways all the way into the city. The goal is to create a network of interconnected natural areas and trails. Such a system will make all the land more valuable.

You can't get there from here: in some places, segments of old railroad rights-of-way and other trails must be connected or rebuilt.

Opposite: Eastbound and westbound lanes should be separated wherever possible. The whole freeway won't be transformed overnight into a roadway like this scenic stretch of I-90 near Cle Elum. But in coming decades, as segments are repaved and widened, the immense rivers of concrete can be split into narrower streams with natural landscaping dividing the lanes. Separating roadways is an important goal of the Mountains to Sound Greenway Trust.

117

The innovative management plan created for Tiger Mountain State Forest protects the quiet beauty of 15-Mile Creek and other watercourses. The greenway won't freeze the landscape forever; it will provide a framework in which change will occur without destroying fundamental values and features.

natural areas change over time, and those in the greenway will be no exception. The greenway won't freeze a geographic region for all time; it will provide a framework within which change can take place without destroying certain fundamental features and values.

To create that framework, we will have to make connections, supply the missing links: trails that miss each other by a mile or two in the Snoqualmie Valley and elsewhere should be joined; even if most people will use only short segments of trail, those segments should be parts of a network. Habitat should be continuous; where large blocks of it are already partly separated by development or physical barriers, the most logical way to connect them is often by preserving undeveloped corridors along rivers or streams. Some of those riparian corridors are already protected, but the protected strips must be wider. The one-hundred-foot buffer required on either side of a salmon stream is too narrow for terrestrial animals. Scientific literature suggests that the minimum corridor width should be three hundred or even six hundred feet. In a developed area, keeping wild animals safe from domestic dogs and cats may take at least a quarter mile. If a corridor will be used by people as well as animals, it will have to be wider than if animals alone were using it.

Master-planned developments in natural areas should preserve trails and wildlife corridors. Trailheads should be established and preserved. New freeway rest areas should provide access to trails and historic sites for people traveling by either car or bus. Signs should tell people what they're looking at. Maps should show land managers—and anyone else who's interested— where critical natural and historic sites are located.

Peaks, ridges, and other highly visible parts of the landscape should all be preserved. Some undeveloped intersections should stay undeveloped;

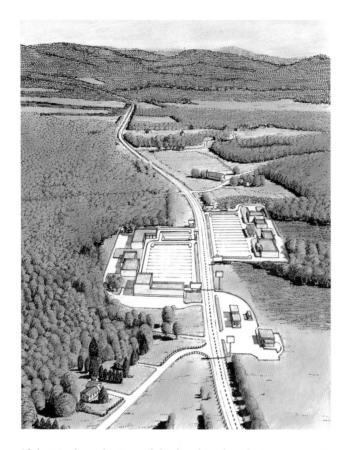 

if that isn't realistic—if the land is already too expensive to acquire for open space—development should be limited in scale and shielded from view. Parcels of land that stand between the road and large natural areas should stay undeveloped, too. A single intrusive building may not make the larger area any less valuable for habitat or recreation, but it can change the aesthetics of the entire landscape. Where a sweeping view from the freeway shapes the character of a vital passage—the first ascent toward Snoqualmie Pass, for example, or the first view west to the Olympics—any new buildings constructed nearby should be sited and designed so that they don't block the view.

Where development already presses up against the road—where the opportunity to build a real greenway has already been lost—the best hope may be a parkway: a road buffered from its surroundings by heavy landscaping and a screen of trees. Realistically, we can't raise enough money to buy existing commercial buildings and tear them down. But we may be able to create transitions to and from areas of true greenway that aren't too jarring, passages through city or suburb that don't totally destroy the feel of the greenway itself. Obviously, planting trees along the freeway is no substitute for preserving forests or farms. But it's better than nothing, and in some cases it's the most that can be done. If I-90 really is the front door to western Washington and a place where many thousands of people spend hours of their lives each week, then providing some aesthetic amenities makes sense. Looking at a screen of trees may be less satisfying that looking at a forest, but it may be more satisfying than looking at a tilt-up concrete wall.

This is not the place to discuss the balance between property rights and regulation. That is a critical issue in our society at this time, and the balance that will be struck by the end of the century is far from clear. The

Design along roadways can make a big difference. The sketch on the left shows conventional development, with buildings set close to the highway. A more creative design is shown on the right. Setting developments back from the road can preserve existing views and the contours of the landscape.

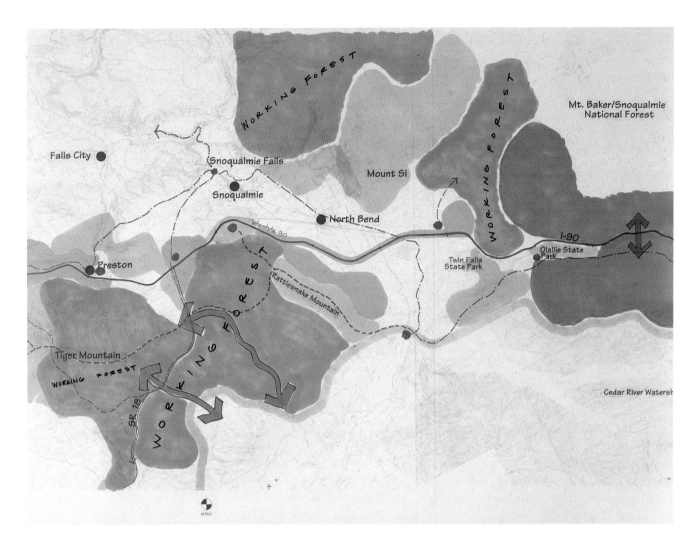

Only a limited amount of land will be set aside as parks or wildlife habitat. Narrow corridors that enable wildlife to move between large blocks of habitat, shown in purple, and working forests, shown in green, will be critical parts of the greenway.

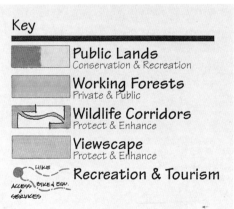

Key

Public Lands
Conservation & Recreation

Working Forests
Private & Public

Wildlife Corridors
Protect & Enhance

Viewscape
Protect & Enhance

Recreation & Tourism

The Mountains to Sound Greenway Trust recognizes that growth will not stop. But future growth can be compatible with the greenway. Where development has already taken place close to the freeway, no one is going to buy the land and tear down the buildings. But we can at least plant trees that will screen the buildings from view. These three renderings of freeway views near Issaquah show the effect that plantings can have. At the top is the present-day view, followed by the views two and fifteen years after planting.

121

Creating ways for walkers and bikers to move in and out of the city is a greenway goal. Preserving the landscape and creating more opportunities to enjoy it will enhance the region's quality of life and attract good jobs and businesses committed to the greenway idea.

Greenway Trust has no desire to get entangled in that controversy. It does not advocate preserving critical areas that are privately owned by forbidding their owners to develop them.

The Greenway Trust wants to see land or easements or development rights bought outright. It wants more exchanges between private owners and the state or federal governments so that crucial pieces can be saved under public ownership. It hopes some private owners will voluntarily transfer easements or development rights to the public. Land already in the public domain should be managed in ways that support the greenway concept. The greenway should be taken into account whenever rest areas are built or roads are widened. New bridges or underpasses should be built so that wildlife and hikers can cross highways without taking their lives into their hands. Wildlife does not like passing through narrow culverts under the roads. Neither do hikers. The body count of elk is substantial along part of I-90, at least one cougar has been killed crossing State Route 18, and the average hiker won't enjoy sprinting to beat an oncoming gravel truck to the far lane.

Where hikers or cyclists have to negotiate city streets, there should be stoplights, wide sidewalks, and, wherever possible, physical barriers to separate them from traffic. Trees could be planted along urban hiking routes. Zoning or design standards could require street-level uses that give the route visual interest. (You can get where you're going by wandering through parking lots or between warehouse walls, but you're not likely to enjoy it.)

Setting visual standards does get into the realm of regulation, which hardly makes it a radical idea. Local governments already regulate land use all the time. The Greenway Trust wants to be sure that local land-use decisions strengthen the greenway framework. If the greenway becomes a regional goal, local governments should use it as a guide and a rationale for their planning. It could give all those separate governments a common vision.

Communities will still control their own futures. They'll be able to add housing, jobs, and businesses to increase their tax bases. Purchases of land and development rights should, however, help to define the boundaries within which those communities can grow. Their own laws and regulations should ensure that the placement and scale of development don't destroy critical habitat, trails, or views. Decision-makers should acknowledge, for example, that the advantage of letting a few people enjoy the views from expensive ridgetop houses must be balanced against the disadvantage of forcing literally thousands of others to look at those houses instead of at the ridge itself.

Again, the idea is not to stop growth. Growth will happen. But it does not have to happen everyplace. It does not have to consume and transform a region in which natural beauty and ready access to natural areas are a significant part of the culture—and the economy. A lot has been written about the "quality of life" that attracts people who help high-tech industries and professional service firms succeed here. In western Washington the natural setting and the ease of enjoying that setting play a crucial role.

Nature also brings the tourists in. Tourism has become big business in Washington. More than thirty million people vacation in the state each year; two-thirds of them bring cash from other states or countries. They come for a variety of reasons, but a 1990 study done for the state Department of Trade and Economic Development found that for most visitors "Washington = spectacular outdoor scenery." It explained that "travelers most often associate Washington with beautiful scenes of grand mountain ranges, lush green forests and interesting coastlines." Tourists don't come to see strip malls or warehouses or fast-food restaurants. They don't come to see tastefully landscaped office parks or residential developments. They come for nature. And it is very much in the region's financial interest to let them find nature: tourists spend more than $2 billion each year in the Seattle–King County area alone. Making this region more like the places tourists come from won't heighten its appeal.

Trees and open space make places more attractive to home buyers as well as tourists. Forest, trails, and wildlife should enhance property values in growing towns. The 1987 Seattle Engineering Department study of the Burke-Gilman Trail found that "about 70 percent of real estate agents and home owners and 88 percent of condominium owners believe that being adjacent to the trail would have a positive or neutral effect on selling a particular property. . . . Newer owners who had recently been in the real estate market were even more positive about the trail. About 88 percent of the home owners and 89 percent of the condominium owners who had bought their properties after the trail was opened felt the trail would have a positive or neutral effect."

In other words, there are economic arguments for saving habitat and trail networks and views. But they are not the main arguments. Creating a greenway makes economic sense, but it is not basically about economics. It is about character and continuity, the uniqueness of place. Tony Hiss writes in *The Experience of Place* that "until recently, when people spoke about a vivid experience of a place, it would usually be a wonderful memory, a magic moment at one of the sweet spots of the world. . . . These days people often tell me that some of their most unforgettable experiences of places are disturbingly painful and have to do with unanticipated loss" (Knopf, 1990).

Many people living in the greenway area have experienced that sense of loss in other places. They have seen hills that they walked and camped on bulldozed literally out of existence for the huge Irvine Ranch development

Nothing will keep commuters off the freeway, and nothing will keep them from moving to more rural communities farther and farther away. It's important to agree on guidelines now, while the eastward spread of population and business can still be channeled into limited areas.

south of Los Angeles, or seen swamps they walked through as children cleared, filled, and paved over in upstate New York.

Almost everyone, it seems, has a stereotypical example of ugliness covering an entire landscape. For some it is Southern California. For others it is northern New Jersey. Closer to home it may be the strip development along Aurora Avenue or Pacific Highway South.

Would current zoning and current sensibilities permit the development of anything quite that garish and seedy along the greenway routes? Not quite. But bulldozers already rip topsoil and vegetation from places that are or could be trailheads, and communities sprawl outward so that the boundaries between them start to blur. Some areas beyond the city have been invaded by development that is visually jarring. In others the threats aren't visible yet, but they are no less real. The historic farms in the upper Snoqualmie Valley, the green fields that separate communities and provide a sense of historical continuity, no longer produce crops or farm income. People don't make a living from their soil. If the land or the development rights aren't bought by a public agency or non-profit corporation interested in preserving the old hop fields and pastures, they will simply disappear. People have already drawn up plans and made investments that may alter the landscape dramatically in the next ten years. Places where the public already owns land or easements will survive, but the interconnections of trails and habitat and the overall feel of the area face an uncertain future.

No one is trying to make the future exactly like the past. That's not the point. The point is that however much other things change, critical parts of the landscape should look and feel as they do now. In time, some may look and feel as they did fifty or a hundred years ago, when the ancient trees still stood.

Ideally one will be able to stand on Mount Si fifty years from now and see a landscape much like the present one: the forested ridges, the open fields, the distinct towns. Cougars and other wild animals will still live on those forested slopes, still follow those dark ridgelines to the edge of the city.

Recreation in the greenway corridor doesn't mean only hard-core hiking and climbing. Tourists come to the Northwest especially to enjoy its natural beauty. These people savor the surroundings while taking it easy on a hot day on the Snoqualmie River.

The remnants of the old Indian trail will have been preserved for future generations; they will really be, in Morris Jenkins's words, "a trail that'll never disappear." Hikers will be able to climb down from Si and follow newer trails to Cle Elum or Elliott Bay. Even in the twenty-first century, there will be some commercial logging and therefore some large commercial forests close at hand. One will also know that coming down from Si, he or she can drive, walk, ride horseback, or cycle through an area that is clearly not Southern California or northern New Jersey or wherever else the archetype of excessive development may be. Whatever happens, the views of distant mountains will remain. Si itself, like the peaks of the Cascades, like the white cone of Rainier, will always be there, largely unaltered, in the background. The challenge will be saving the foreground—which is, after all, the place in which most people actually live.

Mount Si will be there for the ages whether we do anything or not. We must make an effort to save the foreground—the places where most of us actually live.

The Mountains to Sound Greenway Trust

Joanna Buehler
Save Lake Sammamish, Friends of
Cougar Mountain

Curtis Bull
Kittitas County Planning Department

Greg Bush
Metro

Mark Carey
Kittitas County Planning Department

Christine Carlson
National Park Service

Harry Clark
Ellensburg

Sharon Claussen*
King County Parks, Recreation & Open Space
Comprehensive Plan

Michael Collins
Washington State Department of
Transportation

David Conine
North Bend

Dave Crooker
Plum Creek Timber Co.

Joanna D'Asaro
Back Country Bicycle Trails Club

Dan DeWald
City of Bellevue Parks Department

Shane DeWald
Seattle Department of Engineering

Rudy Edwards
Mount Baker-Snoqualmie National Forest,
North Bend District

Bruce Eggleston
Kittitas County Planning Department

Steve Elkins
City of Cle Elum Planning Commission

John Ellis
Weyerhaeuser Co.

Dick Fankhauser
Washington State Parks & Recreation
Commission

Bob Farrell
Puget Western, Inc.

Bill Finnegan*
Puget Sound Power & Light Co.

Suzy Flagor*
Seattle City Watershed

Pat Freedman
Windermere Builder Services
Snoqualmie Pass Advisory Council

LeRoy Gmazel
Snoqualmie

Lori Grant
King County Planning & Community
Development Division

Robert C. Greene
Kittitas County Cattlemen's Association

Don Harris
Seattle Department of Parks and Recreation

George Hilsinger
Washington State Department of
Transportation, District 6

Roger Hoesterey*
City of Bellevue Parks Department

Jack Hornung
Organizer of 1990 Greenway March

Scott Jacobs
Puget Western, Inc.

Morris Jenkins
Cle Elum

Rod Johnson
Washington State Department of
Transportation

Maryanne Tagney Jones
Preston Community Club

David Kiehle
Washington State Department of Natural
Resources, South Puget Sound Region

Dick Kloss
Snoqualmie Pass Sewer District

Leon Kos
Issaquah

Harry Krug
Washington State Department of
Transportation, District 5

Brian Lenz
Puget Sound Power & Light Co.

Kenneth E. Lloyd
Adjunct Professor, Central Washington
University

Bill Longwell
Issaquah Alps Trails Club

Roy Lumaco
Cle Elum Chamber of Commerce

Doug McClelland
Washington State Department of Natural
Resources

Kim McJury
Roslyn City Planning

Bill Melton*
Washington State Department of
Transportation

Judy Moen
Cle Elum

Ted Muller
Washington State Department of Wildlife,
Region 4

Sam Nagel*
U.S. Department of Agriculture, Forest Service

Mike Naylor
Washington State Department of Natural
Resources, Southeast Regional Office

Gus Nelson
Issaquah Alps Trails Club

Charles Payton
King County Cultural Resources Division

Michael Perez-Gibson
Washington State Department of Natural
Resources, Land & Water Conservation

Linda Price
Happy Trails Horseback Riding Ranch

Dick Ryon*
Weyerhaeuser Co.

Dick Sandass
Metro

Hank Sarbiewski
Puget Sound Power & Light Co., Timberlodge
Restaurant

John Savich
Washington State Department of Trade &
Economic Development

Tim Schmidt
Washington State Parks

Sally Sheridan
National Park Service

George Simpson
Cle Elum

Roger Skistad
U.S. Department of Agriculture, Forest Service

Milo L. Smith, retired professor
Central Washington University

Kate Stenberg
King County Environmental Division

Catherine Stephenson
Wenatchee National Forest

Nile Thompson
Puget Sound Railway Historical Association

Nancy Tucker
North Bend

Hartwig Vatheuer
Plum Creek Timber Co.

Greg Watson
Snoqualmie Valley Historical Museum

Tom Wood
Issaquah Alps Trails Club

*Member Steering Committee

Additional Reading

Bagley, Clarence. *History of King County Washington.* Chicago and Seattle: S. J. Clarke, 1929.

Garreau, Joel. *Edge City: Life on the New Frontier.* New York: Doubleday, 1991.

Hidy, Ralph, Frank Ernest Hill, and Allan Nevins. *Timber and Men: The Weyerhaeuser Story.* New York: Macmillian, 1963.

Hiss, Tony. *The Experience of Place.* New York: Knopf, 1990.

Kirk, Ruth, and Carmela Alexander. *Exploring Washington's Past: A Road Guide to History.* Seattle: University of Washington Press, 1990.

Kruckeberg, Arthur R. *The Natural History of Puget Sound Country.* Seattle: University of Washington Press, 1991.

Little, Charles E. *Greenways for America.* Baltimore: Johns Hopkins University Press, 1990.

Prater, Yvonne. *Snoqualmie Pass: From Indian Trail to Interstate.* Seattle: The Mountaineers, 1981.

Washington's Centennial Farms: Yesterday and Today. Olympia: Washington State Department of Agriculture, 1989.

Works Progress Administration. *Washington: A Guide to the Evergreen State.* Portland, Oreg.: Binfords & Mort, 1941.

Index

Boldface page numbers indicate references in captions.

Alpine Lakes Wilderness, 40, 64, 69, 70–75, 85, 105
Bagley, Clarence, 52, 53, 57, 107
Bellevue, 16, 32, 61, 63, 67, 79
Black River, *53*, **60**, 61
Boeing Company, 63, 64
Bogue, Virgil, 40–41
Boyle, Brian, 42, 85, **86**, 111, 112, 113
Buerge, David, 61
Bullitt, Stimson, 82–83
Bullitt Foundation, 87, **89**
Burke-Gilman Trail, 30, 91–101, 123
Burlington Northern Railroad, 91–92
Carnation, **28**, 30
Cascade Range, **21**, 35, 49, 51, 70, 73–75
Cedar River, 15, 26–27, **28**, 31, 39, 40, 51, 58, 87, **89**
Cle Elum, 21–23, 42, 45, 57, 62–64, 67, 98, **117**
Commercial forestry, 14–15, **28**, 31, 47, 60–61, **67**, 73, 79, 103–113, 125
Cougar Mountain, 32, 40–41, 56, **58**, 64, 79–82
Cycling, 13, **16**, 92, 94, 101
Denny, Arthur A., 53, 57, 69
Denny, David, 58
Denny Creek, 21, 26, 69–70
Dept. of Natural Resources (Wash.), 47, 83–85, 87, 98, **108**, 111–112
Development, 22, **44**, 45, **47**, 79, 81, 106, **112**, 118–119, **121–124**

Duwamish River, 53, **60**, 61
East Sammamish Plateau, 16
Easton, **16**, 24, **43**, 98
Elk Heights, 21, **43**
Elliott Bay, **35**, **37**, **125**
Ellis, James R. (Jim), 42, 87
Fall City, 13, 16, 28, 52
Farming, **14**, 21, 30, 56
Farmlands Preservation bond issue, **28**, **94**
15-Mile Creek, **118**
Forest Service (U.S.), 47, 62, 85, **108**, 115
Forward Thrust, 41, 42, 64, 94, 98, 101
Gas Works Park, **92**, 98, **101**
Georgia-Pacific Corporation, 85
Gilman, Daniel, 57, 69, 70, 91, 107
Granite Mountain, 70, 73, 75
Great Northern Railroad, 57
Green River Valley, 31
Grouse Ridge, 27, 34, 89
High Point, 31, 61, 63, 84
Hop Growers' Association, 56
Hornung, Jack, 37, 39, 41
Hydroelectric power, **12**, 58
I-90, 11, **14**, 16, 24, 31, **34–35**, 43, 67, 69–71, 75, **115–117**
Indian John Hill, 21
Indians, 14, 22, 49–52; Duwamish, 53, 61; Snoqualmie, 13, 16, 51–52; trails, 49–51; Yakima, 51–52
Iron Horse State Park, **16**, 24
Issaquah, 21, 31, 43, 56, 84
Issaquah Alps, *see* Cougar, Squak, Tiger mountains
Issaquah Alps Trails Club, 37, 39–41, 82, 84, 87
Jenkins, Morris, 24, 49–50, 61, **125**
John Wayne Pioneer Trail, 16, 24, 75, **76**, 97–98
King County, 40, 58, 82, 87, 89, 105, 107, 111, 112
Kirk, Peter, 57, 70
Kirkland, 28, 57, 63, 70
Kittitas County, **22**, 42, 58
Lake Keechelus, 21, 24, 49, 51, 52
Lake Sammamish, 16, 34, 56
Lake Union, 61, 64, **92**
Lake Washington, 32, 34, 40, 45, 56, 57, 61, **63**, 64, 91
Lake Washington Ship Canal, **60**, 61, 97
Longwell, Bill, 84
Manning, Harvey, 39–40, 64, 79–82, 85, 101, 111
Marymoor Park, 97, 98, 101
Matthews Beach, 91, 92
McClellan, George, **26–27**, 51, 52
McClellan Butte, 26, 27
Meadowbrook Farm, 14, 52
Mercer Island, 32, **34**, 63
Mercer Slough, 32
Metro, 32, 40, 101
Milwaukee Railroad, *see* Milwaukee, St. Paul, and Pacific Railroad
Milwaukee, St. Paul, and Pacific Railroad, 16, 24, 37, 59, 62, 64, 97–98
Mining, 22–23, 32, 56–**58**, 61, 63–64, 70, 79
Mount Rainier, 11, **12**
Mount Si, 13–14, **17**, **27**, 28, 64, 85, **125**
Mount Stuart (Stuart Range), 21
The Mountaineers, 13, 39, 59, 62, 84, 92
Mountains to Sound Greenway, 37, **39**
Mountains to Sound Greenway Trust, **39**, 41, 47, **67**, **71**, **86**, 87, 89, **105**, **117**, **121**, 122
Mountains to Sound March, 37–42, 85

Newcastle, 32, 56, **58**, 63, 64, 82, 98
93rd Street neighborhood group, 91–94
North Bend, 11–13, 15, **16**, 27–28, 51, 107
Northern Pacific Railroad, 53, 57
Olmstead brothers, 34, 40
Olmsted, Frederick Law, 40
Pacific Crest Trail, 37, **38**, 75, **76**
Perkins, William, 52, 56
Pike Place Market, 64, **65**
Pioneer Square, 64
Preston, 16, 31, **44**, 61, 63, 67, 97
Preston-Snoqualmie Trail, 97
Property rights and regulation, 119, 122–123
Puget Sound, 34–35, **101**
Rails-to-trails conversions, 40, 41, 91–101
Raging River, 28, 31
Railroads, 40, 56–57, 59
Ranger's Prairie, 27, 52, 53, 56
Rattlesnake Lake, **16**, 38
Rattlesnake Mountain, 14, 27, 31, 45, 87, 89
Rattlesnake Prairie, 27, 87
Redmond, 28, 30, 67, 97
Reinig, Dionis G., 24–25
Renton, 28, 53, 56–57, 63
Robertson, Harold, 82, 111
Rockafellar, Mamie, 91–92
Rose, Bob, 85, 112
Roslyn, 21–23, 57, 63, 64
Sammamish River, 97, 98, 101
Sammamish Slough, 61
Sammamish Trail, 30, **91**, **94**, 97–101
Seattle, 15, 30, 32, 34–35, 52, 56–59, 64, 67, 91–98, 103
Seattle Engineering Department, 97, 123
Seattle, Lake Shore and Eastern Railroad, 57, 61, 64, 91–**92**
Skiing, **25**, 26, 62, 64
Snoqualmie, city of, 11–13, **14**–15, 27–28, 60, 61, 63, 64, 67, 87
Snoqualmie Falls, **12**–13, 16, 28, 40, 58, 97
Snoqualmie Falls Power Company, **12**, 58
Snoqualmie Pass, 24–27, 37, **38**, 40–45, 49, 51–53, **55**, 58–61, 63–64, 73, 75, **76**, 98, 105, 107
Snoqualmie River, 11–13, **17**, 28, 40, 51, 56, 75, **124**
Snoqualmie Valley, 11, **12**, 14, **16**, 27, **28**, 30, 40, 51, 56, **105**, 118, 124
Snyder, Gary, 51, 103
Squak Mountain, 40–41, 64, 79–83, **103**
State Route 18, 31, 45
Sunset Highway, 28, 45, **55**, 60, **67**
Thomsen, Ted, 37, **39**, 41
Tiger Mountain, **13**, 31, 40–41, 45, 64, 79–87, **108**, 111
Tiger Mountain State Forest, 31, **86**, 112, **118**
Tinkham, Lieutenant Abiel, 51, 52
Todd, Jim, 92, 97, 101
Tollgate Farm, 14, 52
Tolt River, 30
Tradition Lake Trail, 84
Trust for Public Land, 41, 87, **89**
Unger, Stan, 40, 94
Van Bokkelen, Major J. H. H., 51, 52
Washington State Parks and Recreation Commission, **16**
Washington Wildlife and Recreation Coalition, 39
Waterfront Park, 34, 37
Weyerhaeuser Company, 11, 13, 15, 27–28, 60–61, 64, 85, 87, 97, 105, 109, **111**
"Wilderness on the Metro," 39
Yakima River, 21–22, 75
Yesler, Henry, 103
Yesler's Wharf, 34